Wilfried de Jong is a well-known and highly regarded broadcaster, journalist and writer in his native Holland. A familiar face on Dutch TV, he has made a number of award-winning sports documentaries. In 2012 he won the Nico Scheepmaker Award for the best sports book of the year for *Head in the Wind*, which went on to be a bestseller in Holland. In 2015 his collection of cycling columns *Solo* was nominated for the Dutch Sports Book of the Year. *The Man and his Bike* combines the very best of his stories on cycling in one unique collection.

This book is introduced by Bert Wagendorp, columnist at the Dutch paper *de Volkskrant*, chief-editor of the cycling magazine *De Muur* and the author of *Ventoux*.

THE MAN AND HIS BIKE

WILFRIED DE JONG

Translated from the Dutch by David Doherty
Introduced by Bert Wagendorp

EBURY
PRESS

1 3 5 7 9 10 8 6 4 2

Ebury Press, an imprint of Ebury Publishing
20 Vauxhall Bridge Road
London SW1V 2SA

Ebury Press is part of the Penguin Random House group
of companies whose addresses can be found
at global.penguinrandomhouse.com

Penguin
Random House
UK

'Click-Clack', 'Solo', 'A Pulse of 48' and 'Fausto No More' were first
published in *Solo* (2014). 'Mist on Ventoux', 'Munkzwalm', 'Merckx to the
Millimetre', 'Nude With a Wheel', 'Farmer on the Road', 'Cycling Porn'
and 'Front Wheel Spinning' were first published in *De man en zijn fiets*
(2012). 'Hôtel Neuf', 'Stickers', 'Wool', 'Black Feathers', 'Flat', 'Cramp',
'Montalto', 'Bend' and 'Mona Lisa' were first published in *Kop in de Wind*
(2012). 'Jim Shine Fine', 'Bartali's Attic' and 'Addio, Marco' were first
published in *De linkerbil van Bettini* (2005). All first published in Dutch
by Uitgeverij Podium.

First published by Ebury Press in 2017.
This edition published in 2018.

www.penguin.co.uk

A CIP catalogue record for this book is available from
the British Library

ISBN 9781785034015

Printed and bound in Great Britain by Clays Ltd, St Ives PLC

CONTENTS

INTRODUCTION

I FIRST MET WILFRIED DE JONG during the 1990 Tour de France. Or perhaps it was 1991. He was working on an article entitled 'The Sounds of the Tour'. My memory might be playing tricks there too. It could just as easily have been 'The Smells of the Tour'. What I do know is that he had come up with what – to my knowledge – was a brand new take on the Tour. In light of the endless column inches published on the world's premier cycling event, it was a remarkable feat. You'd think that by the early 1990s every possible angle had been covered.

But there's no point airing such views in the company of Wilfried de Jong. Seen through Wilfried's eyes, the world is so rich and varied that there are always new angles to cover. And yes, even in the Tour de France, only a fraction of the possible avenues have been explored. Most of us tend towards a superficial view of the world, a view in which the Tour is simply a matter of winners and losers. Who's on the podium? Who's riding in that coveted yellow jersey? Yet there are individuals for whom reality doesn't stop there. To them our surface reality is a portal to layer upon layer of reality beyond. Wilfried de Jong is one of those individuals. Let's call them artists. They take us deeper, to share in experiences that are sometimes unsettling, sometimes euphoric. We should cherish such minds or risk losing our own to a world of boredom and predictability.

1

* * *

WHEN I FIRST MET WILFRIED at the start of the 1990s, I had known him for quite some time. He was one half of Waardenberg & De Jong, a celebrated duo whose mercilessly madcap theatre shows were the talk of the Netherlands in the 1980s and into the following decade. With partner in crime and fellow Rotterdammer Martin van Waardenberg, Wilfried wove the absurd and the insane into onstage creations that always threatened to burst at the seams. While their work was rooted in the real world, it was abundantly clear that this pair of outlaws were intent on stretching reality to its limits and peering at it from all kinds of weird and wonderful perspectives. To see Waardenberg & De Jong in full flow was to enter a dreamworld in which their every thought, association and mad idea had come to life. Time and again I left the theatre utterly exhausted after an evening spent convulsed with laughter. Later Wilfried confirmed my theory of the creative drive behind the shows: they were born of the belief that chaos and confusion are a rare source of beauty that should never be stifled by an excess of rational thinking.

Chaos and confusion reached a new extreme one fateful evening when Wilfried came crashing to the stage from a height of five metres. A wave of hilarity swept through the audience: this was the kind of stunt only Waardenberg & De Jong could pull off. Until it became clear that we had just witnessed a near fatal collision between fantasy and cold, hard fact. The rest of the tour had to be cancelled and Wilfried spent months recovering from an unnerving collection of fractures.

Once his bones had healed, Wilfried de Jong could have spent the next three decades making show after show, before retiring as an eminent man of the theatre with a bank balance to match. But even the absurd and the insane begin to pall when it's your job to bring them to life on stage night after night. There comes a time when the sparks no longer fly. At least, that's my interpretation of what happened when Wilfried decided to take things in an entirely new direction.

Even at the peak of his theatre career he had found time to make radio shows and write a book of short stories. Now he added television to his repertoire. It gave him the chance to pursue another of his passions: sport. He began with a series called *Sportpaleis De Jong*, and followed that up with *Holland Sport*, quite possibly the best sports show the Netherlands has ever seen. It revealed a new side to Wilfried: the storyteller who lovingly combines words and images in the portrayal of the total dedication shown by athletes. He instinctively understood that top athletes who sacrifice almost everything to achieve a single goal – victory – offer an unrivalled perspective on passion. The artist in Wilfried struck up a unique rapport with these sporting heroes: a mix of admiration and journalistic curiosity enlivened by an irrepressible urge to present sporting passion in the most aesthetically pleasing way possible. Many of the items he made for these programmes – along with the sports documentaries he makes to this day – have become classics of Dutch narrative journalism, thanks in no small part to his inspired long-term collaboration with peerless cameraman Rob Hodselmans.

Wilfried de Jong is also an actor. In this capacity he played a leading role in the film adaptation of my novel *Ventoux*. One of the film's finest scenes came about when Wilfried decided to abandon the script briefly and allowed the real Wilfried de Jong to take over from the character he was playing. Anyone who understood what was going on witnessed a remarkable feat of self-characterisation: a balancing act between fact and fiction, sublimely executed.

The readers of his weekly sports columns in leading Dutch daily *NRC Handelsblad* can count on Wilfried to lend a heightened air of drama and intrigue to the weekend's main sporting events. He achieves this not by distorting reality or resorting to cheap tricks but by zooming in on telling details that come to symbolise a deeper truth that could so easily have gone unnoticed.

IT IS AS A WRITER that Wilfried de Jong unites his theatrical roots with the documentary maker, the sport lover, the columnist and the journalist. Perhaps there's even a hint of Wilfried the jazz aficionado in the capricious rhythms of the tales he tells.

There's a good reason why cycling takes pride of place in Wilfried's sporting prose. For writers from countries with a strong cycling tradition, the sport resonates in the same way as boxing resonates for many an American man of letters: Mailer, Talese and Liebling to name but three. The two sports share a lyrical quality. In both, the dividing line between harsh reality and the stuff of fable is often tantalisingly thin, a feast for the imagination. What you see is not what you get. There is more going on beneath the surface of the visible. Such hidden depths are a gift to writers with the presence of mind to take raw fact as the starting point for the yarns they spin.

Wilfried de Jong is just such a writer, in this collection of stories and beyond. Sometimes he takes on the role of protagonist. The man loves his bike, and I know from experience that even on the saddle he likes to take reality – in our case middle-aged boy racers on pricey cycles – and enrich it as only a natural storyteller can. Join him on a training run and before you know it, you're part of a decisive breakaway in a legendary stage of the Tour de France. In other stories he handpicks his heroes from the broodingly romantic side of cycling's history: Coppi, Bartali, Pantani. He is besotted with Italy, a nation where truth is so often stranger than fiction.

4

Some of his work sticks close to the facts. A story like 'Mist on Mont Ventoux' unfolds without much in the way of embellishment. In others, 'Munkzwalm' for example, his memories take on a new dimension. But embracing the fictional is not the same as twisting reality: by freeing himself from the tyranny of the factual, a true writer can come closer to the heart of the real world and bring to light a fresher, more rewarding reality.

Wilfried de Jong has a deft way with words. His lightness of touch gives his readers every opportunity to engage with and amplify the reality presented on these pages. He has no desire to steer us towards a foregone conclusion. He would much rather see us set off on our own exploration of the fascinating no-man's land between fact and fiction, companions on the endlessly imaginative journey in which he himself takes so much pleasure.

Bert Wagendorp

Click-clack

France

I T WAS THE SIMPLEST OF CAMERAS. A black box with a built-in lens and the word Instamatic along the top. None of us knew what this meant but it suggested that the camera did everything for you. All you had to do was press the button.

Click-clack.

As a boy, I loved taking holiday snaps, capturing the big wide world in a little square frame. The knack was to hold back till exactly the right moment. There were only 24 frames on a roll of film and tradition dictated that one of those had to be sacrificed on immortalising our bleary-eyed departure. The engine of Dad's green BMW 2000 warming up outside our front door in Rotterdam. Mum and Dad in the front, me and my two brothers in the back. By the summer of 1975 my sister had already bailed out and was off gallivanting with her pals.

Roll down the windows, wave at the camera and we were on our way.

Look out, France, here we come.

We knew that the 11th stage of the Tour would be passing close to our campsite in the Pyrenees. The Tourmalet seemed like the ideal spot. All 2,113 metres of it. *Hors catégorie.* On Tuesday, 8 July 1975 we were at the top, ready and waiting.

Almost every detail of the hours we spent on the Tourmalet has faded into oblivion. Looking back is not my favourite pastime. After

Mum and Dad died, the stacks of photo albums from our parental home had ended up at my sister's. It took us ages to unearth the photos I had taken that day. Stuck into a little green album, its spine tattered and torn. No captions, just a bunch of pictures from a long time ago.

The old photos did what old photos do so well. The memories began to come.

We must have left the campsite in Bagnères-de-Bigorre a few hours before the stage was due to start and made the steep drive up the Tourmalet. I seem to remember that Dad's trusty BMW couldn't make it to the very top and we had to pull over with an overheated engine. We walked to the summit and found ourselves a decent spot. I hung the camera around my neck.

The photoshoot of my young life was about to begin.

MY 17-YEAR-OLD SELF, a lanky lad in corduroy flares, face framed by a curtain of hair, points the camera at his parents and brothers sitting in a row. We've brought our own folding chairs. Mum and Dad's even have arm rests.

There's a chill in the air. Dad's a frozen-food wholesaler and used to the cold, but even he has a jumper around his shoulders. I see an inadvertently exposed stretch of shin, pasty-white as always. Mum has her hands clamped between her thighs. My brothers are sporting sun visors. Had the publicity caravan already gone past?

I'm standing at the other side of the road. An oval display on top of the camera tells me how many photos I have left.

In the distance, I can see the caravan crawling up the mountainside. The riders are dots, followed by a column of toy cars. I try to work out how to capture a moving rider with my click-clack camera and decide to aim to the right in the hope that they'll ride into shot.

Cars, motorbikes, blaring horns, loud voices.

That'll be them now.

One by one the riders come within range of my lens. These are the days before helmets and shades. Cyclists still have hair and eyes. They are coming thick and fast. Who is worthy of a photo? I spot the yellow jersey: Eddy Merckx, his hands on the top of the bars. Gloves with air holes. Orange frame. Thin tubes. Cap on back to front. Black sideburns. A face that means business.

Click-clack.

With any luck, I have just immortalised the mighty Merckx. Then again, I might have snapped the blurred hand of a clapping spectator.

Eddy is gone. Quick, time to turn the serrated wheel and move the film on. Riders shoot past. Too many to recognise. I hold my fire.

Who have we here? Luis Ocaña in a Super Ser shirt. The same intense red as his bike. The Spaniard with his furious cycling style, up on his pedals. Across the road, spectators are already straining to see who's coming next. Fools! This is where you should be looking. At Ocaña. Winner of the 1973 Tour.

A Frisol jersey. Dutch team. Who can this be? Well, at least he's a Dutchman. Click-clack. I'll look him up when I get home.

Specs. Gerrie Knetemann. Lagging behind against a medical backdrop: Aspro emblazoned on the car behind him. Headaches were big business even back in the day. Knetemann has grabbed hold of a newspaper to tuck under his shirt on the descent to the foot of the Aspin. Keeps out the cold. As a paperboy, I know the ink will leave its mark. Smudged black words mirror-written on his sweaty torso.

All the riders have passed. Once a stream of back-up cars has rolled through, the mountain grows quieter. I cross the road to join my folks. Who did they spot? I've got Merckx, I'm sure of it. I saw yellow. Fingers crossed that one comes out okay.

· · ·

NOW, ALMOST FOUR DECADES LATER, I have them in my hands again, those little squares of 1975. A photo freezes time but starts a faded film running in your head. They live, breathe, move. I see a carefree holiday. My loving parents. My brothers' faces, still blessed with youth. Family life, the good old-fashioned way.

I take a closer look at the pictures. Sure enough, there's Merckx. And Knetemann. And Ocaña, who went on to take his own life in 1994. Put a gun to his head and pulled the trigger. Could that young Frisol lad have been Henk Prinsen? A white jersey, let's see, must be a young Francesco Moser. And is that Francisco Galdós in the blue-and-yellow KAS shirt? Colours of the past.

These days phones take photos. Meanwhile Hipstamatic and Instagram provide filters to make our digital snaps look older than they really are. Why this hankering for yesteryear? Is Merckx on steel still somehow closer to our dreams than Wiggins on carbon?

I remember taking my holiday snaps out of the envelope at the chemist's the week after we arrived back home. Those images of my cycling heroes had been playing on my mind for days and there they were at last, spread out before me on the counter. My Instamatic had done me proud. The life of a cyclist reduced to a still image on a square of photo paper.

I recall looking down at Merckx. Proudly, fondly. At the top of the Tourmalet, he had passed me at a distance of just a few metres. Back home a special honour awaited him. The man who went on to lose in 1975 – his yellow jersey snatched away by Frenchman Bernard Thévenet – would spend the next 39 years stuck in my tattered green photo album.

MIST ON MONT VENTOUX

France

SNOT. I HAD TO CLEAR MY BUNGED-UP NOSE. Nothing but my right hand for a hankie. Oh well … One blast and my nostrils were open again, fresh September air tingling behind my eyes. I shook the snot-green slime from my fingers and glanced to the side. The valley was already a fair distance below me. The first five kilometres of Mont Ventoux were in the bag. Around 15 minutes' cycling.

I took a swallow from my front bottle and the bland taste of sports drink lingered in my throat. Alongside me was my back-up car: an airport rental with my ten-year-old son Sonny in the back, hanging out of the window.

'The gradient here is six per cent, Dad. And soon it'll be ten.' His tone was calm and even, a newscaster summing up the day's atrocities for the viewing millions.

'Right, thanks,' I said. My bottle was back in its holder.

Ventoux veterans back in Holland had warned me. Six kilometres in, a hairpin bend veers left and the steep climb begins in earnest.

Another 100 metres to go.

They don't call Mont Ventoux the Giant of Provence for nothing. At almost 2,000 metres, it's by far the highest peak in the region. I had yet to see it in all its glory. When we set out from the village of Bédoin, a stubborn bank of cloud had settled on the summit.

My knees pumped up one after the other. And sank towards the asphalt just as fast. Looking down between my legs, I saw my chain driving the small chainring and the third lightest cog: 34 teeth up front, 23 at the back. I could still change down to 26 and 29. Two more chances to ease the pain as the going got tougher.

Another 50 metres till the next gear change, right before the hairpin.

. . .

THIS CLIMB WAS MY GIFT TO MYSELF. I'd hit the big Five-O. More a milestone than a birthday. Inviting the folks round to OD on cake and crisps wasn't going to cut it. No, what I needed was my bike and the company of a few good friends. Benny and Rob had agreed to come along for the ride. Two men looking on from the comfort of a rental car, bearing witness as their pal worked himself into a sweat conquering the Ventoux.

Benny was happy to go along with anything as long as there was a slap-up meal in the offing. So here he was, at the wheel of the brand-new Renault we had picked up at Nice airport. Rob was in the back with Sonny. Not exactly his bag, cycling. He'd rather be out pounding the pavements of his home turf in Amsterdam on his weekly run.

Sonny was guest of honour at this strange celebration of mine, recording the spectacle with his own mini camcorder. His plan was to edit an official birthday movie on his computer when we got home.

The Renault was already rounding the bend, Sonny's head still sticking out of the window. I watched his face disappear behind the boulders.

Just time for another slug to quench my thirst. I grabbed the bottle and gave it a squeeze. A thick stream shot into my mouth.

Too much. The excess liquid splattered on the asphalt and I realised it could well be the one gulp I'd be crying out for on my final kilometres to the summit.

I heard the car change gear. As if I needed reminding that things were about to get steeper.

Though I was sticking to the outside of the bend, I could feel the tension in my thighs increase in a matter of metres. My tempo was plummeting. Ahead of me lay the notorious forest where many a dismayed Sunday cyclist is forced to dismount after miles of hard labour. The trees reminded me of the sparsely wooded banks I once planted for my model railway as a boy; after smearing glue either side of the track, I scattered grit on the sticky patches and dotted them with a handful of plastic pines for my locomotive to chuff past.

My back-up car had slowed and was back alongside, Sonny capturing every second of my first metres through the forest in glorious close-up. A photocopy of the gradients per kilometre was stuck to the folding table in front of him.

'Dad, this is the forest, right?'

I nodded and panted.

'It'll soon be ten per cent,' he said cheerily, as he continued filming.

I changed gear and my legs heaved a sigh of relief. The chain was now turning 26 at the back. Six kilometres of Ventoux behind me, another 15 to go, but I still had something in reserve.

In the 1970s, there was a gifted Belgian climber by the name of Lucien Van Impe. A man born to cycle up a slope. Six times he was King of the Mountains in the Tour de France. As soon as the road started to rise, you would see Van Impe easing his way through the peloton, supple as can be. I remembered him leaping off his bike at the end of a soul-destroying mountain stage, fresh as a daisy. As a microphone was shoved in Van Impe's face, the team mechanic took care of his bike. The little man with a greasy rag hanging out of his back pocket looked at the cassette and saw that Van Impe hadn't even used his lightest gear. There wasn't a trace of grease on the cog. 'Lucien's in good form,' he announced triumphantly to the camera crew. 'His 22 is still clean as a whistle!'

I was determined to keep my 29 clean for as long as possible. It's a simple mind game. Steer clear of your last resort and you're still one helluva guy, every chance you'll make it to the top. No way was I going to downshift and leave myself nothing to fall back on. That would mean giving up. And giving up was not an option. Unthinkable. I'd never be able to look my friends or my boy in the eye again. And least of all myself ...

I managed to regain some kind of control over my breathing. The steep road ahead meandered lazily through the trees. Not a flat section in sight, only the promise of worse to come. Ten per cent gradient for metres on end.

'Bonjour, ça va?'

I just about jumped out of my skin. My front wheel lurched half a metre to the right.

A sturdy bloke with a cheeky grin almost brushed against me as he chugged past, maintaining an enviable tempo.

'Oui, oui,' I panted.

Sweat trickled over the close-cut hairs on his neck and into the collar of his light yellow shirt. I frowned at the word printed on the back. Cacahuètes. The tin of peanuts pictured below provided the translation. Pillock! What cyclist worth the name would wear a shirt extolling the virtues of peanuts? A rider couldn't wish for worse fuel. Impossible to grind down and swallow. Too dry, too fat, too salty.

With every turn of the crank, he moved ahead by a good 20 centimetres. I gave myself a stern talking-to. Don't let him get to you, stick to your own pace. He might be pushing a bigger gear. Let Peanut Brain do his thing.

Ten per cent. Well over twice the gradient of the ramp leading up to the Van Brienenoord Bridge back home in Rotterdam, which I'd tackled on many a training run. The closest thing to a mountain stage in my flat-as-a-pancake part of the world.

REWIND TO THE PREVIOUS EVENING. To Sonny and I sharing a king-size bed in a hotel in the village of Mazan, 15 kilometres from Mont Ventoux. It must have been around ten. Benny and Rob had retired to their rooms after dinner in the hotel restaurant. Sonny's head was peeping out from under the bedclothes, camcorder and stopwatch beside him on the bedside table.

He looked at me drowsily.

'Dad, why do you have to climb that mountain anyway?'

'Because it's one of the toughest to climb.'

'So why not pick an easier mountain?'

'I just want to see if I can get to the top of this one.'

'And what if you can't?'

'Then I'll be really annoyed with myself, but that's okay.'

'So it's not really *that* important after all.'

'Uh ... I just liked the idea of cycling up a really high mountain on my 50th birthday.'

'But wouldn't it have been much easier to do it on your 20th?'

'Yeah ... you have a point there, son.'

The desire to climb a mountain is a bid to defy gravity. There's a good reason why civil engineers do their damnedest to stick to the valley. It's only when there's nowhere else to go that the asphalt starts creeping up the mountainside like a tendril of ivy.

Cramp is often the price a cyclist pays for a demanding climb. And then there's the nightmare scenario: the heart sending up a distress signal. Suddenly death can be around the next bend. It's the fate that befell British rider Tommy Simpson. During a stage of the 1967 Tour, within striking distance of the Ventoux summit, Simpson fell exhausted from his bike. He begged onlookers to help him back onto the saddle, only to swerve across the asphalt in the scorching heat and finally collapse. The Tour physician was soon at the scene but his valiant resuscitation attempts were to no avail. Simpson died in the helicopter on his way to hospital. Alcohol and amphetamines were found in his bloodstream.

Simpson's death is a warning to all riders who push the human body beyond its limits. But let fear get a foot in the door and you're lost. There is no reaching the top of Mont Ventoux without pain. It takes guts to attack a mountain. To refuse to let nature cut you down to size.

* • * • *

APART FROM THE DRONE OF THE RENAULT'S ENGINE, the forest was quiet. Even the sound of birds among the trees had died away. Peanut Brain was a long way ahead. He heaved himself out of the saddle and stood on his pedals.

I ploughed on at a steady 11kmph, keenly aware of the need to keep pressure on the pedals or risk wobbling out of balance.

Twenty-nine teeth. One flick of my right hand and the going would get a little easier. No! Don't do it! Breathe in, stroke, breathe out, stroke, breathe in, stroke, breathe out.

Peanut Brain was still up on his pedals. No man could keep that up in this forest. In this ruthless woodland chill that saps the strength from your muscles.

A fly landed on my arm and started rubbing its front legs together. Lazy hitcher. Nerves rattled, I blew in its direction but it took the gust in its stride and stayed put. The little bugger had to go. I huffed and I puffed and watched it fly off into the trees.

'How many kilometres on the clock, Dad?' Sonny shouted from the car, a few metres ahead of me.

I pressed a button on my bike computer.

'Six-point-three!'

All quiet in the car. I saw Sonny bow his head and pictured him frowning at the figures in front of him, working out the route and the increase in gradient.

A can by the side of the road caught my eye. I recognised the crumple of green and blue. Sprite. Way too sugary for the Ventoux. It'll only make you thirsty.

Sonny stuck his head out of the window again. 'Ten per cent coming up!'

It was like my own son was personally ratchetting up the steepness of the road. I was pedalling much harder than I had been a minute ago.

'How long?' Two words. All I could manage.

'What?' asked Sonny.

Breathing heavily, I waited for the moment when I could add another word to the question.

'How long ten?'

His head disappeared inside the car.

I was doing around 9kmph.

Come on, kid. It's not rocket science. Just run your finger down the column. How long? How long ten?

'I think you'll be back down to nine per cent after one kilometre, Dad,' I heard him shout at last.

My eyes began to focus on the little black stones that made up the surface of the road. It seemed smooth but there were a few millimetres of space between each stone. Zoom right in and I was riding from stone to stone, on thin air. I shook my head. Keep this up and I'd convince myself I was riding on cobbles.

I yanked my front bottle from its holder and took a few mouthfuls. Liquid heaven. The breath I missed swallowing them down nearly did for my rhythm. It was all I could do to keep the bike under control.

I shoved the bottle back in its holder.

My pace continued to wobble. No let-up. The road kept on rising. Time to change down to 29? No! Under pain of death!

Asphalt and trees. Nothing but asphalt and trees. Still no sign at all of the summit.

* * *

AS WE'D SET OUT FROM THE CENTRE OF BÉDOIN, a couple of cyclists had come hurtling down the road, rain jackets flapping. Back from the top. Their faces were deep red, lips caked with dried spittle.

'*Froid?*' I asked, pointing at the hidden summit.

'*Ça va, ça va!*' they yelled, with a gesture that could have meant anything.

It was September. The walls of the bike shop in Bédoin where I had pumped up my tyres were hung with huge photos of Mont Ventoux cloaked in white. They showed cyclists being stopped by a gendarme, the barrier lowered across the road. The mountain pass was *fermé*. Even in months when you least expected it, Mother Nature could give us mere mortals a rap on the knuckles.

'You're going to make it, Dad.' Sonny's head had popped back out of the car window. 'You've got your lucky magnet with you, right?'

I ran my hand over my back pocket and felt the metal disc tucked between two gel packs. I gave him a thumbs up.

* * *

18

THE RABO TEAM'S MOST GIFTED RIDER, Robert Gesink, powered up one of the Ventoux's less steep ascents during the 2008 Paris–Nice stage race. His astounding cadence had drained the fight from all the climbers in the leading group by the time they reached the village of Malaucène. Only Australia's Cadel Evans was able to latch on to Gesink's back wheel and went on to beat the Dutchman in the final sprint.

Marco Pantani cycled up Mont Ventoux alone, ahead of the rest in the 2000 Tour de France. With a gut-wrenching effort, Lance Armstrong in the yellow jersey reeled the Italian in. Side by side they battled up the final stretch to the top. The two of them maintained a punishing pace. Pantani with his light, agitated bearing and supple tread on the pedals. Alongside him the manic American cycling machine, eyes squinting slightly in his pale, gaunt face. In the end, it was Pantani who inched his wheel over the line to take victory. Afterwards, the American liked to be reminded of how generous he had been that day. After all, the win could just as easily have been his.

Gesink, Evans, Pantani, Armstrong … I had to stop thinking about pros. From this day on I was in my fifties. A sporting sad sack with a bee in his bonnet: to prove he was still strong enough to make this climb. An old fart out to show his son he still had a tough guy for a father, not some couch potato brushing crumbs from his paunch in front of the telly.

'Are you okay?' asked Sonny, after a long silence. 'It's another six kilometres through the forest.'

Six kilometres. I thought of my regular training route around Rotterdam and imagined the flat road rearing up at a ten per cent gradient.

'Yeah. Tough.'

'What does your meter say?'

'It says 13.7.'

'Okay, that makes the gradient ... 8.7 per cent.'

The landscape had hardly changed. I seemed to be cycling the same stretch over and over, stuck in a perpetual motion machine. Forever cycling, never finishing.

'No ... hang on ... ten per cent,' came the voice from the car.

I blew a drop of sweat from the tip of my nose. Took another swallow from the bottle. Already three-quarters empty. I had to stand out of the saddle to keep my rhythm going. When I sat down again it felt like someone pulling on my shirt.

Friction? I peered down at my front wheel; the brake pads were well clear of the rim. And at the back? No, nothing wrong there either.

Push yourself too far in the Ventoux forest and you'll pay for it later. Or so they say. I had to stay within my limits. Otherwise I'd never make it.

I contemplated holding on to the car for a second. Skipping a single turn of the pedals. Bliss. It would make all the difference to my legs, to my head.

The next bend was approaching. Was this where the gradient began to ease off? I looked up to see a man at the roadside, hunched over his bike. A man in a yellow shirt. Cacahuètes had caved! Peanut Brain was done for. I knew it! Start too quickly and pay the price. A damp patch had formed beneath the tin of peanuts on his back, sweat was dripping from his flushed face. As I drew level, I spotted a puddle of sick on the asphalt at his feet. The same colour as his shirt. I'd seen better ads for peanuts.

'Bonjour!' I yelled, with all the good cheer I could muster. It left me short of breath but it was worth every gasp.

Cacahuètes looked up, startled, and I gazed into the hollow eyes of a desperate man. Gobs of peanut yellow around his mouth.

He didn't say a word. I didn't look back.

I had settled into a decent pace. Magnificent forest. Sublime asphalt. Twenty-six teeth turning nicely.

'It's nine per cent here, Dad.' The car was back alongside me.

Only nine? Bring it on! I was ready for anything after seeing the self-satisfied grin wiped off Peanut Brain's face.

A row of big block capitals flashed beneath my wheels. LANDIS. Letters painted on asphalt stick around a long time, long after the name they spell has sunk into obscurity. For a few years, people had gathered here to cheer on America's Floyd Landis as he made this climb in the days before his doping ban. A fan had lugged a bucket of paint up the mountain to leave these six letters in broad brushstrokes ahead of the stage. Landis: no doubt there would soon be a place for him again in the forgiving peloton.

I looked up. The sky had clouded over. I was glad I'd remembered my arm-warmers in case conditions turned cold and blustery on the final stretch. I had left the valley sporting my fire-engine red Acqua e Sapone kit, the height of summer cycling fashion.

The forest was thinning out and I began to see through the trees. Not much in the way of distractions. No deer in flight, no marmots scampering for cover. Should I be breathing more deeply to keep my oxygen levels up?

The Renault had been crawling up the road beside me for at least an hour, in first gear. Benny must be about to lose his mind behind the wheel.

One more kilometre to go till Chalet Reynard, a car park and restaurant at an altitude of 1,440 metres. Ventoux veterans had told me this was the first spot where the hard climb lets up a little. A chance to catch your breath before the six-kilometre slog through the lunar landscape to reach the summit.

Benny upped his speed a little as he drove past. Was he planning to settle down in front of me?

Then came a dry, scraping sound.

'Fuckin' hell.' Benny's voice.

One of the car's front wheels had slid off the edge of the road and was jutting out over a deep ravine.

'Sonny!' The danger hit me in a heartbeat. 'Sonny, out of the car! Now!'

Sonny opened the rear door and hopped out onto the asphalt, followed by Rob. They stood together at the side of the road.

Where was Benny? Still in the car?

No. He was out too, walking over to join Rob and Sonny.

I kept on pedalling, though my pace had slowed.

'Keep going, Wil,' I heard Rob shout. 'We can sort this.'

'Are you sure?' I yelled over my shoulder. 'Is Sonny okay?'

'Yep, we're fine here. Keep going.'

'Okay. See you at the top,' I shouted, and cycled on.

A car with a French number plate came down the mountain, an older man at the wheel and a woman in the seat next to him. I waved furiously at the driver to slow down. Thankfully, he complied.

As I rounded the next bend, our Renault came into full view and the impact of what had just happened slapped me full in the face. One more metre and the car would have gone over the edge.

Rob had yelled at me to keep going. But did he realise the car was that close to the brink? A simple shift in weight could send it plunging into the ravine.

I kept on pedalling, though my pace continued to slow. The French car had stopped at the scene of the accident and the man and woman were talking to Rob and Benny, gesticulating wildly. No sign of Sonny.

The road was still rising but my mind had disengaged. My legs were churning away at the pedals. That was all. Every chance I got, I looked down through the trees, hoping to catch a glimpse of Sonny. The Frenchman was now on his knees, peering underneath the Renault. More gesturing ensued.

My computer read 14 kilometres. Another seven to the summit. If the cloud lifted, it might only be another one till I set my sights on the white-topped peak with its famous observatory, that plucky middle finger thrusting skywards.

The summit was up there waiting. What good would it do to turn back now? A man my age could be forgiven for taking a little break, resting one foot on the road. But turn back? I had never given up on a climb before.

A fuse blew in my brain. I could almost smell scorching. What was wrong with me? What kind of bastard cycles on and leaves his ten-year-old son at the scene of an accident, at the edge of a ravine?

My legs stopped pedalling. I was still in two minds but my handlebars were already lurching to the left. My front wheel made an about-turn.

The descent was a piece of cake. It felt strange not to have to pedal any more. In a matter of seconds, my speed leapt from 7 to 30kmph, and on up to 50. I had to brake to take the hairpin bend with the requisite care.

I screeched to a halt next to the Renault. Sonny was still standing where I had left him, at the roadside overlooking the ravine. Camcorder in hand. Perfectly calm.

I unclipped my shoes and felt terra firma under my feet for the first time in what felt like an age. I left my bike on the inside bend and walked over to Sonny, legs trembling at the transition from cycling to walking. My thighs felt fat and heavy.

'Everything okay?'

Sonny gave me a thumbs up. Not a trace of fear.

'So you've stopped then?' he said.

This was true. I had stopped.

Rob, Benny and the French couple were standing in the middle of the road. The underside of the rental car was badly scraped. The left front wheel was hanging in midair.

'How do you plan to get her moving?' I asked.

'If a couple of us hang off the back of the car and someone puts her in reverse, that should do it,' said Benny, still visibly shaken. 'With any luck it will shoot back from the edge.'

No one made a move. Everyone was unharmed. Suddenly this was all about salvaging a stupid rental car. I wanted to get back on the bike. Get moving again. Moving like I had never stopped.

'I'll get into the car,' I said. 'Key still in the ignition?'

'Yup,' Benny said.

Sonny was fiddling with the buttons on his camcorder. I left him to it; as long as he stayed put he'd be fine.

Carefully I slid into the passenger seat of the Renault. It felt strange to be operating a car from this position.

'Start her up,' Benny shouted, 'then release the handbrake and put her from neutral into reverse.'

I started the engine and the three men hung from the back of the car with their full weight.

'I'm releasing the handbrake and going straight into reverse. Okay?'

'Okay,' came the reply.

'Here goes,' I shouted above the noise of the engine. I slid the gearstick into reverse and gave a little touch on the accelerator. The engine strained and pulled the dangling wheel back onto the asphalt. Back in her element, the Renault immediately began to roll backwards.

'Brake! Brake!' Benny yelled.

The car began to pick up speed as it headed downhill, veering left and right. From the passenger seat I only had one hand to steer with. Try as I might, I couldn't get my left foot to connect with the brake.

My leg was shuddering. I could hear the tyres slipping.

This was not going well. The rental car was out of control and I began to steel myself for the inevitable.

'Brake!'

My foot found the brake at last. I hit the pedal as hard as I could and the car went into a skid. I looked over my shoulder. My last tug on the wheel had set the Renault on a collision course with the French couple's car. I tried to change direction but too late. Eyes closed, I braced myself for a bone-crunching impact.

Another metre or two to go.

The cars collided with a dry smack and our Renault came to a halt at last.

Everyone came charging over.

My eyes searched for Sonny. He was still standing at the road-side, camcorder at the ready. I put on the handbrake and jumped out of the car.

'All right?' I asked.

'Why didn't you brake, Dad?'

'I tried but I couldn't hold her.'

'Yeah, well, this stretch is 9.7.'

The skid marks were clearly visible, a black zigzag across the full width of the road.

The French couple, Rob and Benny were standing by the cars, looking bewildered. The collision had been full-on, but there was barely a scratch on the paintwork. Only now did I notice that the Frenchman's car was exactly the same model as our rental. Their identical flat hatchbacks had been the only point of impact.

'We should have thought that through a little better,' Benny said.

Sonny was standing next to me. I tousled his hair with my gloved hand.

The French woman was staring sniffily in the other direction. She wanted out of here. I knew the feeling. Her husband was having another gander at the back of his car.

Time for a spot of entente cordiale. *'Mon anniversaire, moi cinquante, Mont Ventoux avec mon fils et maintenant … boom.'*

'Ah oui,' she said with an air of polite indifference as she watched her husband get down on his knees and continue his inspection.

'This could have been very bad indeed,' Benny muttered.

'Yeah, if the car had gone over the edge we'd have been in real trouble,' said Sonny with a grin.

Rob, Benny and I looked at each other. Our relief was tangible.

'Well, if it's all the same to you lot, I'll be on my way.' Without waiting for a response I set my bike back on the asphalt, jumped on and clipped my shoes into the pedals.

* * * * *

I WAS UP AND RUNNING AGAIN. The going was easier than before my U-turn. As if my body had been fitted with a fresh pair of legs. As if a masseur had kneaded out the fatigue and the fright.

I had to eat something. I reached for one of the gel packs tucked into the back of my jersey and my fumbling fingers brushed against a small metal disc. A magnet with a picture of St Christopher, patron saint of travellers, grabbed from the steel ashtray of my old Mercedes at the last minute. Sonny's idea. 'It'll bring you luck, Dad.'

I tore the pack open with my teeth and sucked out the contents. A bitter gel with a caffeine edge. I stuffed the empty pack in my pocket and took another few gulps from my front bottle. Empty.

Here the road was less steep. I was even able to change up a couple of gears. Not much in the way of greenery; I would soon be above the tree line. I rounded a gentle bend and saw a restaurant up in the distance: Chalet Reynard, closed by the look of it. The road had been widened to provide paying customers with a parking spot.

Beyond the cover of the trees, I felt the full force of the wind. The cold was setting in and I pulled up my arm-warmers. Another 100 metres and my journey through the moonscape would begin.

Here the road took another upward surge. One six-kilometre ascent to go.

The famous yellow-and-black markers on the valley side of the road slid past. Was that the sound of the Renault's engine coming up behind me? I looked back and saw Benny at the wheel, still with a troubled look in his eyes. He drew level. Sonny rolled down his window and stuck his head out again. His cheeks were flushed.

'The final kilometre is 11 per cent, Dad,' he said.

Scraps of mist came floating towards me. My breathing grew heavier. Up on the pedals. Back on the saddle. Up on the pedals again. I had to battle into the strong wind. The world around me dissolved in the mist. Benny switched on his headlights. Through the open window I heard him say to Rob, 'Bloody dangerous. I can hardly see a thing.'

It grew weirdly dark. At 3.30 in the afternoon I was suddenly on a night ride to the summit. I could only see 20 metres in front of me.

The car dropped back.

'You're going to make it, Dad,' I heard Sonny yell before the sound of the engine faded and I was left alone with the rushing of the wind and the sound of my own panting.

Those 29 teeth had gnawed their way back into my brain. No! Mustn't give in! But then ... why not? Go on, why prolong the suffering? Change down! The chain connected with the lightest gear. My last resort. It helped. A little.

I fished a second gel pack from my pocket, squirted the contents into my mouth and gagged. Up here you had to survive on water and air alone. Adrift on this barren sea of stones, that would have to be enough. I spat out half the gel and took a couple of glugs from my second bottle.

There was no view. No sign of the summery Mont Ventoux I had seen in the revolving rack of postcards back in Bédoin: a man in shorts and hiking boots peering through binoculars into the valley where the steeple of a village church rose modestly to the sky. A pile of picturesque rubble in the foreground. *Bienvenue à La Provence.*

Visibility was shrinking fast. Ten metres now, if that. How far to go? Hang on, my running total was wrong. Shit! I'd forgotten to subtract the distance I had doubled back.

I sucked in air. There was definitely less oxygen at this point. I had seen pros strap on an oxygen mask after reaching the finish. My wheels were spinning frantically in a giant helium balloon.

I heard a car coming up behind me. I looked over my shoulder and saw two old-fashioned yellow headlights approaching. A 1960s-style Citroën was spluttering up the mountain in the mist, the driver's nose almost pressed against his fogged-up windscreen. He was wearing a short-sleeved cycling jersey. I turned to focus on the road ahead. Where exactly was I in this moonscape?

The Citroën beeped its horn. A tinny sound. The glow of its headlights lit up my straining calf muscles. I looked back again. The man behind the wheel was sweating like a pig. He wiped the condensation from his windscreen with the front page of an old *L'Équipe*; I recognised the bold red letters. He reminded me of Tommy Simpson. Hollow eyes set in a long face. Cycling cap slapped comically back to front on his head.

The car's bumper nudged my back wheel. I jumped and almost keeled over. I heaved myself out of the saddle, struggling to keep my balance. The headlights projected a vague shadow and I watched my own elongated body bobbing up and down in the mist, my head disappearing into the murk. An idiotic sight. I couldn't tell if the drop at the end of my nose was snot or moisture from the air.

The driver was now hanging out of his side window. His neck stretched impossibly until his mouth was right next to my ear.

'Please, put me back on my bike. Put me back on my bike,' he whispered.

I smelled booze on his breath.

'Can't,' I said, gasping for air.

The Citroën's engine sounded like it was ready to explode. Its RPMs were through the roof. It didn't pass me, though I was down to 8kmph.

We swerved across the asphalt, he in his old banger, me on my bike.

'How far?' I asked.

The driver shook his head, sweat beading on his brow.

The ravine had to be down to my left. To the right I could make out a few heaps of pale yellow stone. Beautiful and ugly at the same time. My life had been reduced to two turning pedals.

Behind me the Citroën coughed and shuddered to a standstill. The engine went dead.

The driver repeated his plea. 'Please. Please, put me back on my bike ...' His voice faded to nothing. Silence.

I looked to the side. Through the mist I saw a phantom clambering up a flight of stone steps on his knees, steps littered with water bottles, beer cans, gel packs. In among them were photographs, handwritten notes. The wind seized a flap of cardboard and sent it flying. 'Miss you, Tom,' it read.

The phantom crawled on in hope of reaching a raised marble slab that bore the outline of a cyclist. A shining memorial, wet from the mist. The ghostly shape tried desperately to drag himself onto the plinth but his strength failed and his shoes slid out from under him.

With the last of my breath I screamed. The sound carried further than I expected through the blanket of mist.

'Tommy!'

There was no reverberation, no echo. I clenched my fist and raised it at the marble slab. To spur him on. To spur myself on.

Fuck it, Tom. Take a slug from my bottle. Pop a pill if you have to. Let's face it, we've all been there. Come on, one last push together. I won't let you down. I'll shield you from the wind. Your wife is waiting at the top with sandwiches and a flask of hot tea. We're nearly there.

The monument was swallowed by the mist. I spat on the ground.

Altitude does strange things to a man.

I left Tommy behind and fought on alone. Solo. No more respite to be had from my gears. Another turn to the right. Pressure clamped around my legs. Twenty-nine teeth sank into the chain. Chew. Spit. Chew again. Straining. Panting.

At last, I knew where I was. Sonny had warned me. 'Eleven per cent, Dad.'

Sonny. Where was Sonny?

This was the last bend before the summit. Up on my pedals. In the grip of a gale.

There was no finish. Only blank white mist.

Keep going. This mountain had to end. A line had been drawn somewhere. Eleven per cent. One more than ten. Two more than nine. I had to keep pushing.

Hang on. This was getting easier. And easier still. Was this the summit? My legs were speeding up. This had to be the summit. I refused to brake till I was sure the climb was over. Twenty-one kilometres later and here I was: the top of Mount Ventoux. Almost two kilometres high. I got off my bike.

The wind was strong and bitterly cold. Mother Nature flexing her muscles.

The Renault appeared out of nowhere. Benny shut off the engine and Sonny hopped out and ran up to me. Two fogged-up lenses where his eyes should have been. Even so, I could tell he was happy.

'We didn't see you finish because of the mist,' he said.

I leaned my bike against a low wall and realised it was probably the only thing that stood between us and a precipice. I took my son in my arms and soaked up his warmth.

'What was your time?' he asked.

'About two hours,' I replied.

'You can subtract seven minutes for the accident. I timed it on my stopwatch.'

'Great,' I said.

Time, what of it? Time made no sense, not here, not now. All that mattered was feeling my boy's body against mine, so young, so full of life.

'You made it, Dad.'

I smiled. 'I did, didn't I?'

'With a break, of course,' he added drily.

I put the kid down.

At the edge where you can gaze out across Provence on a clear day, there was a metal pole with a sign. SOMMET DU MONT VENTOUX 1910M.

So this was it. My 50th. On a mountain with no view. A gale to blow out my candles. I had earned my place in the league of old men who had battled their physical failings to reach the top of Mont Ventoux. 'Happy birthday, you old tosser,' I mumbled.

I looked down at Sonny and saw him shiver.

'Cold?'

'A bit.'

I buttoned up his jacket and pulled on the windbreaker Rob had thrown my way.

'Time to go down,' I said.

Me on the bike, Sonny tagging along behind in the rental car.

I descended in twilight.

Tommy Simpson was back on the saddle of his stone bike, eyes fixed on the summit. Another kilometre and a half to go but enough food and drink at his feet to see him through.

It was only when I reached the deserted restaurant of Chalet Reynard that the visibility started to improve. I turned to the right and plunged back into the forest.

A black skid mark flashed beneath my wheels. Even as I pointed at the asphalt, I wondered whether Rob and Benny back in the Renault really needed reminding.

'So you've stopped then?' Sonny had remarked.

Couldn't argue with him there. Yes, I had stopped. Time had stood still.

It was fine, though. I would come back next year, I decided. To conquer Mont Ventoux without stopping.

The trees sped past as I tucked in low. My hands trembled on the drops. I hurtled down the mountain, picking up speed in the steep sections. The wind blew tears into my eyes and at one point I saw the counter reach a blurry 85.1kmph.

I had no time for fear. I was on my maiden flight from the moon back to Mother Earth.

Hôtel Neuf

France

THE WEBSITE ALMOST HAD ME DROOLING. Hôtel Neuf. The promise of designer rooms in a newly renovated chateau. A prime location in first-class cycling country. And last but not least ... an outdoor jacuzzi.

A long day's drive over French toll roads took me all the way to Languedoc and by 9.30 in the evening I was within a stone's throw of the castle grounds. I rolled down my window and breathed in the air of the region. Dry pine needles. A dirt track with vineyards stretching away on either side brought me to a closed steel gate where a sign instructed me to drive right up to trigger the opening mechanism. The gate juddered and jolted its way to one side and I drove on at walking pace, taking in the chateau's pale walls and faded gold-fringed awnings. Welcome to the nineteenth century.

A doorman tapped his fingers to his peaked cap by way of greeting. His burgundy jacket was roomy around the shoulders and made him look smaller than he really was. I nodded politely and he directed me to a parking space under a row of gigantic trees. Expensive cars with number plates from Germany, Belgium, Luxembourg, the UK. I couldn't help but notice the distinct lack of low-slung sports models.

A porter came charging down the path. *'Bienvenue à l'Hôtel Neuf. Votre valise, s'il vous plaît?'*

I only had one suitcase in the boot, ten kilos at most, and truth be told, I'm not fond of flunkies. I'd much rather do these things myself while I still can. Nothing worse than that sinking feeling as you fumble in your pockets for a halfway decent tip.

Too late. The porter had already yanked open the boot and laid claim to my luggage. I toddled up the path behind him like a lapdog. He too was sporting a burgundy jacket one size too big. Perhaps the owner was hoping his staff would grow into them.

'The *patron* will be with you shortly,' he said in French. 'I will take your case up to your room.' He trotted into the open lift and turned to face me as the doors slid shut.

The lobby was dominated by a white grand piano. Two photo albums lay open on top. I gave in to the temptation to flick through the photos and captions. A blow-by-blow account of the entire renovation.

The chateau had been bought by a wealthy French family in around 1950, the owners of a once venerable textile firm a few miles down the river. When the industry collapsed, the company went under and the family moved on in search of greener pastures. The chateau had been half-empty all through the 1960s and the abandoned sections soon went to rack and ruin. In 1969 the last member of the family closed the door behind him, leaving the key in the lock in the unlikely event that anyone might want to cross the threshold.

A photo dated 2001 showed the deplorable state in which current owner Christian and his wife Coco found the place when they first visited. Captions handwritten by Coco – the i's dotted with flowers were a bit of a giveaway – sketched the scene: 'On 14 March, Christian and I stood on the ramshackle terrace of the chateau. The front doors were hanging off their hinges. We could simply wander in. The first impression was dreadful.'

I browsed further. One page featured a photo of a wonky WC. 'Even the fossilised turds in the toilet pots did not deter Christian,' Coco quipped.

The next page showed the man himself pointing glumly at his crotch. 'Christian's trousers shredded by a rusty old nail in the wall.'

Once my eyes had stopped rolling, I couldn't help but be impressed by the blood, sweat and tears that had transformed a festering old ruin into the swish hotel I was standing in.

'Welcome to Hôtel Neuf, *monsieur aah … de Pays-Bas.*'

The proprietor himself had sidled up to me. I recognised his pointy face and off-centre specs from the photos, though he had grown a good deal crustier in the interim. His corduroy slacks were burgundy but too small for him if anything.

'Leibnitz, I'm ze owner of zis beautiful pleezz.'

Since all his staff spoke French, why did this Swiss bloke feel the need to give his spiel in English?

'Follow me,' Leibnitz said.

'Merci beaucoup,' I replied.

We walked over to an oak desk where everything lay ready: the check-in form and an antique-looking key with a cuddly gnome attached. Room 214.

'In your email you said you plan to cycle? You are in luck – tomorrow will be a beautiful day. My wife Coco has already mapped out ze route for you. She asked me to apologise for her absence. Zis evening she is selling her homemade bramble jam at ze village fête.' Leibnitz threw a pink sweater over his shoulders and knotted the sleeves loosely in front of his chest. 'Allow me to accompany you to ze lift.'

Leibnitz pressed the button and we both gazed up at the illuminated number above the closed doors. The number 2. It seemed in no hurry to change.

'It's not ze quickest of lifts,' said Leibnitz, and gave a little whistle as if summoning a disobedient dog. It didn't help.

Agonisingly slowly the lift doors slid open. Leibnitz lunged past me and punched a button.

'Zzere you go,' he said. 'I wish you a wonderful stay in our beautiful hotel. Your room is on ze second floor.'

* * *

WITH THE LITTLE GNOME NESTLING IN MY PALM, I strode down the hallway to my room. I opened the door, felt for the light switch and a ceiling light came on. The flunky had laid my case neatly on a bespoke luggage rack.

Kicking off my slip-ons, I scanned the room and blinked. Gnome-patterned wallpaper, a giant toadstool for a table and a duvet cover that looked like a forest floor. I eased open the door to the bathroom and flinched. Two life-sized lady trolls were staring back at me, holding up a mirror. I took in the surreal sight of my horrified reflection flanked by those monstrous faces. I undressed, brushed my teeth, took a piss and whipped my wang to the side for a second to hit the troll closest to me full on the nose.

Sweet Jesus, I had booked this room for two nights! I recalled Madame Coco's arty-farty online ramblings about each room having its own unique *ambiance*. Now the penny well and truly dropped.

A pointy nightcap was waiting for me on the pillow. I chucked it on the floor and turned out the light. As I slipped into bed, I just about jumped out of my skin: there was something hairy between the sheets. I threw back the duvet and slammed on the light to find a cuddly female hobgoblin grinning up at me.

I should've known there would be something fishy about a four-star chateau called Hôtel Neuf. Hotels named after their location are a safe enough bet: Hôtel de la Poste, Hôtel Belvédère, Hôtel de la Gare. But Hôtel Neuf? What was I thinking? Back home I'd never even think of booking into 'The New Hotel'. Now I understood why this lavish place only got four-star reviews and not five. Hôtel Neuf was a fabulous body that reeked like a tart's windowbox.

Without a word of apology, I booted my goblin girlfriend out of bed.

• • •

AT BREAKFAST I TOOK A GOOD LOOK AROUND. Senior citizens, wall to wall. Had I missed something when I'd checked out the hotel website? The man at the next table was holding a sachet of sugar over his teacup. No need to shake, his trembling hand was doing all the work for him while his wife took mouse-like nibbles from a slice of baguette. By the window were a pair of 70-year-old ladies wearing identical summer dresses, a fetching shade of beige. Two for the price of one. The old girl facing me carved her croissant into bite-sized chunks and forked them into her mouth one by one.

Over in the corner I spotted another loner. A man in his forties, I guessed, sporting Ray-Bans. A cap with an unfamiliar logo sat loosely on his mop of reddish-brown curls. He was tucking into a large omelette with a spoon, elbows leaning on the arms of a wheelchair.

The waitress saw me wave and bustled brightly over to my table.

'*Bonjour.* Your room number please, *monsieur*?'

I jiggled my gnome at her.

'*Ah oui*, the gnome room. Number 214.'

I nodded the gnome's fat little head, crossed my eyes and puffed out my cheeks. The girl glanced around and leaned towards me. 'You could do a lot worse, believe me.'

'Impossible,' I said.

'Would you rather have the bat room? Black from ceiling to floor, including the sheets and the toilet paper?'

I conceded. 'Anything more manly on offer, *mademoiselle*?'

'In that case, may I recommend the knight's room? Swords above the bed, shields on the ceiling, chainmail on the walls.'

I crossed two fingers in front of my face. *'En garde!'*

I had the irrepressible urge to act like a youngster around her.

'Hot coffee or weak tea?' she grinned.

'Acorn coffee?'

She looked over my shoulder at the door and her face slumped back into senior citizens' mode.

'Fine, coffee coming up, sir.'

I heard slow footsteps coming up behind me. The return of the Pink Jersey.

'Did you sleep well, Mr Cyclist?'

'Great, thanks. It's like living in a fairy tale. Grimmer than Grimm.'

The Pink Jersey beamed and tightened the knot in his lamb's-wool sleeves.

'I will tell my wife Coco zat ze décor meets wiz your approval. She will be zzrilled.'

He continued his tour of the tables, to make sure his distin-guished guests were all breakfasting to their satisfaction.

*   *   *

BACK IN MY WOODLAND GROTTO, I lay down on the unmade bed. After a moat of French coffee, two croissants with Coco jam and an omelette, I had to loosen my belt a notch. Remote in hand, I indulged in a spot of channel hopping, eventually settling on a black-and-white film on RAI Uno. A teen rebel was racing over the Rome ring road on his scooter. The speedometer in close-up read 95kmph. The boy hit the gas and reared up on his back wheel. As he passed a bunch of pals, he pulled the key out of the ignition and waved it in the air, still balancing on one wheel. His pals went wild. The boy stuck the key back in the ignition, started the engine and landed on his front wheel.

'Yeah!' I exclaimed from the comfort of my bed.

A girl with a fringe not quite obscuring her dreamy eyes walked up to the boy once he had screeched to a halt. She clamped her hands to his cheeks and gave him a long, slow kiss full on the lips. The camera spun around them.

I hopped on. Eurosport was showing a repeat of a regatta. I tucked a second pillow under my head and tried to make sense of the boats on the screen. A mind-numbing spectator sport without a proper finish line. My eyes drifted down to goblin girl sprawled on the floor. I picked her up by her little legs and held her in front of my face. I swear I saw mockery in those eyes. I gave her a swift left to the jaw. She sailed through the air, flopped against the wall and tumbled behind the television.

I turned down the volume and watched as the two young women on the screen fought to control their boat on the wild water. One of them hung overboard in a kind of trapeze, her back almost touching the waves. Hard work. There wasn't an ounce of fat on her body. These were top-class athletes.

My legs were still stiff from the car journey and my body was itching to get moving. My hand slid over my belly. No six-pack, not even close. But compared to the rest here at Hôtel Neuf, I had the physique of a young god. Not much of an achievement. That lot couldn't exercise for 15 minutes unless a nurse was standing by with a defibrillator.

* * *

MY EYES OPENED TO A FLASHY car gliding through an ad man's wet dream. I blinked at the clock below the TV screen. 11.30. I'd been dead to the world for almost two hours.

Time to get my arse into gear. My bike was still boxed in the coffin strapped to my car roof. Once the preserve of skis or the corpse in a tacky B-movie, I had recently discovered that a bike would fit snugly too, minus wheels that is.

I picked up the receiver on the bedside phone and pressed 9.

'*La réception, bonjour.*'

'*Madame Coco?*' I asked in my best schoolboy French.

'Yes.'

'*C'est chambre 214.* I'll be down in a few minutes to pick up the cycling route, okay?'

'Yes, very nice. *À bientôt.*'

I slid off the bed and got dressed, opting for a cycling shirt I had ordered online: brown and sea green separated by a horizontal white stripe with the word GALIBIER, an ode to the towering Alpine summit conquered by Tour de France riders since 1911. I felt sure the folk of Languedoc would appreciate the gesture, given the French sensitivity to tradition. Especially their own.

I left the hotel through a side door and headed for the car. Stretching to click open the ski case and lift out the frame, I noticed a man in the Nissan parked alongside staring up at me. Belgian number plate. No language barrier. He rolled down his window and poked his head out.

'Those plastic things these days weigh nothing at all, eh?'

If I had a euro for every time I've heard that one.

'I ride on steel,' I answered sniffily.

'Never afraid you might fall? One stone in the road and – whoops – you're a gonner.'

'Some people are found dead in their bed,' I replied.

Silence.

I lifted the frame over my head and placed it carefully on the ground. Then I took the wheels out of the boot and began to screw them into place.

'Well … uh … have a good trip,' said the man.

'Merci.'

I walked the bike back to the hotel and leaned it against a wall by the entrance. Just grab the route and I'd be off.

Madame Coco was at reception, hovering over a little table laden with jars of jam and asses' milk soap.

'Ah, zerr you arr,' she cooed, waving a copy of a local map on which the cycle route was marked. 'A lovely trip of around 40 kilometres, mapped out by one of ze waiters in our restaurant. He's a local and he knows his cycling. Not too hilly, not many cars and beautiful scenery.'

I traced my finger along the line, drawn in red felt-tip.

'Oh, and one more zzing. I took ze liberty of mentioning your sporting endeavour to another guest, Mr Collins. He would very much like to accompany you.'

I couldn't help but frown. For me, cycling is a solitary pursuit. The only exception was joining a few of my Rotterdam pals for a circuit along the River Rotte once in a while. We knew each other's strengths; we liked to go at a fair old lick and break away from the group every now and then, but never with the aim of leaving the others behind. Pace-wise we were pretty evenly matched. A stranger's company was the last thing I needed.

'Mr Collins is ready and waiting in his room on ze ground floor,' Coco continued. 'He asked me to call him if you were amenable. If so, he will meet you at ze door in a few moments.'

She must have seen I was having my doubts.

'Oh, do not worry zat you will not understand him. He is an American.'

An American. Oh joy. On one of those ugly Trek bikes, I was willing to bet. Or a Ridley. A pro I knew used to swear that a Ridley frame is made from old heating pipes. Bikes devoid of all style.

41

I took a deep breath and exhaled slowly and silently through my nose.

'Okay,' I said.

Madame Coco nodded. She picked up the phone and keyed in a number.

'*Bonjour,* zis is Coco calling. It's all right. You're welcome ... Okay, bye.'

She hung up.

'Mr Collins will meet you at ze chateau entrance in a few minutes. Have fun.'

I went outside and saw the two old biddies with matching dresses peering at my bike. One of them had my bottle in her hand and was sniffing the spout suspiciously. She jumped when she saw me approaching.

'Oh, we wondered where you were. Do you mind if I ask what's in it?' she said, shaking the bottle. They were Dutch, sisters by the look of them.

I pulled the bottle from her hand. 'An isotonic sports drink with a select hydration system formulated for the optimum replenishment of minerals lost due to exertion.'

'Oh ... it smelled a little bit like lemon juice,' she countered bravely.

'Not likely. Spring onion with a dash of coriander and a smidgen of saffron.'

The ladies exchanged discombobulated glances. 'Ah, I see,' said my interrogator, tugging at her sister's sleeve. They toddled off into the garden arm in arm.

A terrace lay between the hotel entrance and the car park. Every one of the guests lounging in the shade had their head turned in my direction. What? Never seen a man on a bike before?

A voice boomed out behind me. 'Hi, I'm Fats!'

I recognised the cap as soon as I turned around. So this was Mr Collins. A man with no legs. He was sitting in a bucket seat, flanked by two chrome-plated wheels.

I shook his gloved hand.

Fats was wearing an oversized sleeveless T-shirt with the word HELL splashed in gory capitals across his chest. His hands were resting on two circular tubes that he used to turn the wheels. A narrow frame extended forwards from his seat with a small swivel wheel at the end.

'Let's go!' Fats yelled. With a smooth sweep of the arms he set his wheels in motion and sped off through the gate.

We were halfway down the drive before I caught up. I was determined to act as if there was nothing out of the ordinary. Just two regular blokes out for a cycle, only one had no legs and was powering away with his arms.

'We turn right here,' I said.

The names of the villages we would pass through were already lodged in my brain. And if my memory let me down they were folded away in my back pocket on the A4 sheet Coco had given me.

The narrow asphalt road took us through rolling countryside. The farmers had bound their hay together in big round bales that dotted the landscape.

Just as well Fats was wearing sturdy gloves; he was pushing himself hard, churning furiously at the tubes attached to his wheels. Two gear levers were suspended directly in front of his unshaven chops.

We hit a more even stretch. The road was quiet. No harm in cycling abreast of each other.

'You're up for it today,' I said.

Fats looked straight ahead with a deadpan expression. 'How d'you mean?'

'I mean you're fairly cracking along.'

'What did you take me for?' he snapped back. 'Some legless wuss who'd rather be sat on a cushion sipping tea with those bitches back at Hôtel Neuf? Come off it!'

He shifted gear and began to accelerate. I took a look at my computer: 33kmph. Surely a blistering pace for a handcyclist?

This was an American made of the right stuff: open-minded, no need to beat around the bush.

'Car accident?'

'Nope. IED on the road to Jalalabad. Taliban motherfuckers.'

And I thought I was straight to the point …

'Where you from?'

'Buckeye, Arizona. Not far from Phoenix. You know Gila National Forest? Always used to head out there on my mountain bike when I was home from Afghanistan. In the days when I still had fucking legs. Moose, bear – they felt like friends when I was up on those tracks. Used to camp up there sometimes.'

Fats wasn't even out of breath.

We cycled through a village and I recognised the name from Coco's map. Past the village square we would hit a stiff climb. Six per cent up to a forest.

'Things are going to get steep in a bit,' I said, knowing it would be a punishing stretch for Fats.

In the distance I could already see the asphalt rising.

'*Allez, allez!*' shouted a man by the roadside. He was wearing dirty overalls and wiping his hands on a rag.

'*Allez* yourself, French fucker!' Fats growled.

We began our climb. Fats's bike was swinging from left to right and his T-shirt was soaked in sweat. He had slowed to walking pace. I took one hand off my handlebars and placed it on his back.

'No pushing, fucker!'

'Sorry,' I said, and quickly pulled back my arm.

Fats was determined to make the top under his own steam. And he did. As soon as we reached the crest of the hill the road swooped down the other side. He shifted up a gear and gave a fanatical spin on his wheels. Within seconds he was flying downhill in a no-holds-barred descent, throwing his full weight into the bends. I took another peek at my computer: 62kmph.

The man was officially nuts.

As a school-leaver, I had spent six months working in a care home to save up enough money for a holiday. One of the residents was a blind man from Suriname, a double amputee, legs eaten away by diabetes. The man was indomitable. He would barely tolerate my help and his arms had taken over much of the work from his missing legs. They would easily take him from his bed to his wheelchair. One of the few things he couldn't manage was going to the toilet and part of my job was to help him. It was the first time I had seen stumps: black balloons knotted at the end.

Fats's hair-raising descent was over and we were cycling side by side again.

'After I'd recovered from the blast, I took part in a couple of marathons,' he panted. 'Boston, New York. What a sham. Had to start half an hour after the runners and still finished ahead of them. God, the organisers hated that. Not to mention the commentators! There they were waiting for some skinny Kenyan on his long legs and I'd come whizzing by on my hot wheels. The panic on their faces when I rocked up to the finish line! Ha-ha. Motherfuckers.'

Fats had biceps to rival my thighs. I had to keep my pace up not to be left behind. Every now and then I ducked behind his broad back to stay out of the wind, like a track rider digging in behind a sturdy pacemaker. In formation, we cycled through the heart of the next village. Fats clearly didn't believe in braking and I peered anxiously ahead as we sped down towards the main crossroads. Thank God there was nothing else coming. I looked up to see the customers outside the local bar-tabac staring at us, hands held above their eyes like sun visors.

As we passed a field of sunflowers, Fats waved his right hand and steered towards the side of the road. When he had lost enough speed, he bumped up onto the verge and put on his handbrake.

'Another effect of the blast: I'm always having to take a leak. Everything down there is shot to fuck.'

At a discreet distance, I took up position behind Fats at the very edge of the road. He wriggled to the edge of his bucket seat and fiddled with his flies. After a bit of a wait, his bladder began to empty. More of a dribble than a stream.

'Weird. It feels like a fire hose about to explode and then this is the result.' He dribbled on.

What was there to say to a legless man taking an awkward leak at the side of the road?

'Watch you don't piss on your shoes.'

I saw Fats's back shudder. Then he began to roar with laughter. He tucked away what was hanging out of his baggy pants and, with a few odd jerks of the hips, settled back in his seat.

Before I knew what was happening, the handbrake was off and he was back on the road.

Drawing level, I looked down to see a smile on his face. 'I like your style, motherfucker,' said Fats. He raised his hand for a high five. I slapped my palm resoundingly against his glove, only to realise it was far from dry.

The day was turning out to be a scorcher. I pointed out a yellow-white swallowtail butterfly, fluttering from plant to plant and sticking its tongue into purple flowers to suck out the nectar.

'Not a bad little life,' I mused. 'Fluttering around the countryside, having a little drink in the sunshine.'

A second butterfly approached the same flower. I wasn't enough of a lepidopterist to know whether they were a couple.

'And they don't grow old either,' Fats replied. 'Seems like a good deal to me.'

He sucked noisily on the transparent tube attached to his bottle. Blue liquid defied gravity and disappeared into his mouth. His nectar.

'Are you staying at the hotel alone?' I asked.

Fats nodded. 'Stayed there three years ago too. With my wife. She was crazy about the red wine they make around here. Bitch is rid of me now. Couldn't handle being hitched to the guy with no legs.'

I watched his Adam's apple bob up and down as he took another slurp from his bottle.

'Sure, she was the devoted wife for the first few months. Wheeling me around, helping me into the bath, shampooing my hair. But, like I said, down below there's not much left. She was gone within the year, shacked up with an army buddy of mine. Dick on legs.'

Fats stared holes in the bushes ahead of him. The butterflies had vanished. A bumblebee circled the empty flowers, too timid to touch down on the narrow landing strip. It buzzed off at high speed.

'What about you? Alone too?'

'Alone here, yeah. My wife stayed at home. She has to work.'

Fats looked at me. 'Good deal, eh? A few days' cycling without her bending your ear the whole time. Is she smart?'

I nodded.

'A looker too, I'll bet.'

I nodded again. 'Yeah. Legs up to the rafters.'

'Fuck you, man.'

ON THE LAST SECTION OF OUR CYCLE, I settled in behind Fats and wondered where he got the energy. Apart from the climb at the start, the speedometer barely dipped below 30kmph the whole route. Did he have dreams where he still walked tall? Did he suffer from phantom pain? The more I looked at Fats's arms, the more I began to see them as legs: hairy legs with elbows as bony knees, wrists for ankles and feet with freakishly long toes. He might be a dribbler but this was a man of steel packed into half a body.

We turned onto the dirt track that led up to Hôtel Neuf and rode right up to the automatic gate. It didn't budge an inch. Apparently the system only responded to car tyres. I rang the bell on the wall and the gate jerked open.

The chateau and its grounds were just as we had left them. The doorman in his burgundy jacket raised his fingers to his cap as we cycled past. Fats saluted in return, his jaw set like an officer, chin up, shoulders back, hand rigid. Only the click of his heels was missing.

I clipped one shoe out of my pedal and slowed to a halt in the car park. Fats stopped too. The terrace up ahead was still packed with guests. A waiter was serving the two ladies in identical dresses. Two cups of tepid tea, no doubt. No one had spotted us.

On a sawn-off tree trunk next to the entrance, the girl who had served me breakfast was having a fag on the fly. She wiggled her fingers by way of greeting, looking even more beautiful than she had that morning.

Fats saw our exchange. 'I Feel Good', he sang, letting rip with a James Brown yelp.

'Thirsty?' I asked him.

'I could murder a Heineken,' he replied.

Ah yes, bog-standard Dutch Heineken – a rich man's drink in France. I signalled to the breakfast girl. She crushed her cigarette under the ball of her foot and walked our way.

'We'd like to order something,' I said. 'Or are you finished for the day?'

'No. What can I get you?'

'Heineken. Bottles,' said Fats, holding up two fingers.

Convinced that Fats was up for it, I decided to put in another request. With the briefest of winks I added, 'Would you mind bringing them over to the jacuzzi?'

She hesitated. 'We're not really allowed to serve bottles at the jacuzzi.'

'And you're not really allowed to smoke in front of the entrance either,' I said.

She flashed me an impish grin and put her finger to her lips.

Fats raised his hand in a vow of silence.

The girl nodded and walked off to fetch our drinks. Balancing on the balls of her feet, she seemed to float with every step.

'Great chick,' said Fats.

The jacuzzi was around 100 metres further along in the garden. A path led straight there, except for a short final stretch across the lawn. I clipped back into my pedals and began to cycle. True to form, Fats was not about to be left behind and began churning furiously at his wheels. We whizzed past the dozing crowd on the terrace.

Fats hooted like a klaxon.

'Attention, attention!' I yelled.

The old folks stiffened in their chairs. One of the identical sisters dropped her saucer on the grass.

We cycled down the path, crossed the lawn and stopped at the jacuzzi. I got off my bike. Out of the corner of my eye I saw Fats struggling out of his seat. I held out my arms but he was having none of it and hoisted his body forwards. It was only when he saw the awkward step up to the jacuzzi that he relented, throwing his arms around my neck like a helpless monkey. I heaved him up the steps and lowered him into the water.

* * *

THE JACUZZI WAS A FAIR SIZE. Fats and I could sit opposite each other with room to spare. He peeled off his T-shirt. I followed suit. GALIBIER and HELL lay next to us on the grass like a cut-up cycling poem.

The control panel next to my head looked perplexingly high-tech. I pressed a few random buttons and felt hard jets of water pulsing against my back. An explosion of bubbles erupted under Fats, who feigned wide-eyed innocence.

'Must be the garlic,' he chuckled, fanning the air.

'Your Heineken, *messieurs*. I'll charge them to Goblin Grove.'

The girl dangled the two beer bottles above our heads. It felt like a game at the fun fair. We grabbed them greedily.

'Join us, baby,' yelled Fats, pushing his luck. She shook her head.

'Sorry, but some of us have trolls to dust.' She sauntered off across the lawn towards the chateau, balancing the empty tray on one hand.

I pressed another button with the rim of my beer bottle.

The jacuzzi began to bubble. Fats's stumps drifted up to the surface and I saw how badly the skin had healed. A mess of proud flesh.

'I'll be here tomorrow afternoon,' I said. 'You?'

Fats was quiet for a moment. 'Love to, man, but I've got a room booked at some swanky hotel in Normandy. Off to see the white cliffs and where the Allies stormed the beaches. Then on to the American cemetery. Figured I should see all those white crosses with my own eyes at least once in my life.'

He threw his head back and disappeared underwater.

I heard footsteps on the lawn and recognised the uneven tread of the Pink Jersey.

'Every-zzeeeng to your liking?' he asked.

'You bet,' I answered.

Fats rose spluttering to the surface.

'May I ask you in future to refrain from cycling on our lawns? Zzzey have only just been dressed. Oh yes, and please do not leave ze jacuzzi on zis setting too long. It uses a lot of power zis way. *Merci.*'

The Pink Jersey unknotted his sleeves. They hung limply on either side of his paunch. He swung around and marched off.

Fats watched him go. 'Motherfucker. Let's crank this thing all the way up to ten.'

'Yeah, all this and more for only 200 euros a night,' I said.

I pushed every button I could find. The water seethed and steamed. Fats yanked off his shorts and tossed them in the direction of his bike. Not to be outdone, I did the same. The churning currents lifted our pale bodies to the surface.

We floated there like a couple of water babies.

STICKERS

New York

WITH THE BUZZ of the metropolis came the joys of anonymity and I decided to leave the curtains open. I hadn't seen a soul at the windows of the lofts across the street from the hotel.

Just as I was pulling on my black cycling shorts, there was a knock at the door. It was one in the afternoon. It couldn't be the chambermaid. I had only just checked in.

'One moment, please!'

Hurriedly I tugged up my shorts, slapped the braces over my shoulders and opened the door.

An older woman with an Indian complexion stared at me over a trolley packed with cans of pop, bags of nuts, and bars of nougat and chocolate. She had a red dot on her forehead.

'Welcome to Hotel Thompson. You want ice?' she said with a smile that was straining at the edges. She drummed the lid of a white bucket with her long fake golden nails.

Nope, no ice for me.

Before I shut the door she slipped a dark cube and a piece of paper into my hand: the order form for tomorrow's breakfast. Irish oatmeal, home-made granola, smoked salmon, skimmed milk.

I didn't even want to think about tomorrow. I had landed at JFK Airport only hours ago and today was to be my first day cycling the streets of New York.

The cube turned out to be a brownie. Complimentary goodies courtesy of the hotel. The label read BAKED JUST FOR YOU, MY PRETTY. PRODUCT OF THE FAT WITCH BAKERY.

I slipped on my cycling jersey and tucked the brownie in my back pocket. A compact cure for any hunger pangs along the way.

* * *

ONLINE I HAD HEARD GOOD THINGS about a bike rental place downtown on West Street. Sure enough, a storefront sign proclaimed BICYCLES in big letters. I hopped out of my cab and went inside.

Helmets and locks took up most of the walls in the cramped space. Three city bikes were leaning against the counter, with two chrome-plated scooters for company. A young guy with a shaved head sauntered up to me, wiping his hands on a frayed oil rag.

'Do you rent real bikes?' I asked.

'And by real you mean …?'

'It's just that at home I ride a racing bike.'

He laughed. 'Welcome to hybrid city.'

Hybrid. Dear God, a city bike masquerading as a racing bike. A two-wheeled transsexual.

The guy gestured for me to follow him outside. A racing bike stood gleaming against the wall. This was more like it. 'Bottecchia' in bold letters on the down tube. Ambrosio carbon rims.

He saw me salivating and shook his head. 'Sorry, pal. My bad. It's my apprentice's bike, not for rent. He's a sucker for Italian frames. Like you, it would seem. It's our hybrid or nothing, I'm afraid.'

My tormentor slipped past me and disappeared through a steel trapdoor and down a ramp, emerging a little later with a bike from the basement.

I checked out the hybrid. Biria, not a make I knew. A sturdy model, designed to take anything the Big Apple could throw at her. Thick tubes, broad tyres, mudguards front and rear, ten gears and straight handlebars. It was the saddle that made my heart sink. Broad and beige, with a hole in the middle. A ladies' bike.

'Is this all you've got?' I said, giving two slaps on the saddle.

'One size fits all.'

The guy went behind the counter and handed me a sheet of paper. The small print helpfully informed me that I had to return the bike in one piece and the store wasn't liable for anything if I went flying over the bonnet of a car. While I signed my life away, he made a copy of my driver's licence.

'Helmet? Basket? Lock?' he enquired.

A helmet on a bike without balls? A basket? I wasn't off to plunder Macy's. No need for a lock either. My plan was to circle Manhattan within a couple of hours.

A boy who had just wandered in asked for 'free air'. His wish was granted. He pulled the hose from the wall and pumped up his tyres.

Free air.

The idea of paying for air struck me as surreal. But then this *was* New York. At JFK I had seen a slogan plastered on the side of a sightseeing coach: ENJOY YOUR 2-HOUR TOUR MORE: FRESH AIR IN OUR BUS.

Was it really possible to filter the filthy air of Manhattan and blow it through a bus?

The shop guy topped up my tyres.

'Right then, I'll be off,' I said.

I wheeled my rental bike through the bustle of West Street and headed for the adjacent bike path. The two-lane route was a long green stripe on my map. Class 1. The best a man can get. It ran along the Hudson, from the south of Manhattan to the north.

I climbed on my hybrid and settled into a halfway decent rhythm. My first few metres on a bike in New York. Exhilarating stuff. Here I was, part of the traffic in a metropolis made for speed. A paradise for taxi drivers tearing down the avenues at 80kmph, while beneath them subway trains shot through their tunnels like rattlesnakes.

To my right, southbound motorists were locked in a no-holds-barred battle to reach the Holland Tunnel as quickly as possible. To my left the Hudson was rippling in the sunshine. I inhaled the river: briny with an edge of waste oil and dead fish. The familiar port smell I knew well from back home in Rotterdam. Before my arrival, these waters had battered the quays of Manhattan. For days on end, the eastern seaboard of the United States had been in the clutches of Hurricane Irene. Entire stretches of coastline had been flooded, but New York got lucky and emerged relatively unscathed.

I was still at odds with my rental bike. The saddle was uncomfortable and too low into the bargain. With every stroke of the pedals, my thighs rubbed against the plastic. The bike lane was too busy with cyclists and joggers to simply stop, so I swerved wide to pass a man lugging excess kilos of wobbling fat under the blazing sun and came to a halt at the edge of the asphalt with one foot in the grass. I turned the handle under my saddle and raised it a couple of centimetres. As soon as I took off again, I could feel the added pressure I was exerting on the pedals.

The New York heat was punishing. I was glad I'd remembered to slap on some sun cream at the hotel. I vaguely recalled seeing 'Factor 30' in a little circle on the tube. Protection enough.

Looking right at the end of every block gave me a tantalising peek into the heart of Manhattan: 30th Street, 31st Street, 33rd Street. The stoplights were on my side, three greens in a row. Along 34th Street I could make out the highest reaches of the Empire State Building. Was anyone looking down at me through Observation Deck binoculars from a height of 1,250 feet? A tiny man on a bike, charging along the Hudson. In a hurry by the look of him.

A bare-chested young man overtook me, riding a hip fixed gear: compact, straight handlebars, frame sprayed light-grey, wheels with extra-broad rims and beige tyres. He was upright on the saddle, thumbing a text message as he cycled. He settled in ahead of me and I saw an eagle tattooed across the breadth of his back. The feathers of the outstretched wings were picked out in different colours and glistened with runnels of fresh sweat.

I clicked the gear lever on my handlebars to 6 and pulled up alongside him. He must have been doing around 30kmph.

He looked up.

'Hi,' he said.

'Hi,' I replied.

He was still cycling hands-free.

'How long can you keep that up?' I enquired. 'No hands?'

'My record is from Canal Street to 125th Street.'

'Impressive.'

His thumbs darted across the keys. It was a long message.

He turned to me briefly.

'Where you headed?'

The green line on my map ran along the Hudson all the way to Inwood, one of Manhattan's most northerly districts. 'Up to Inwood, then back downtown,' I said, trying to sound as casual as possible. 'And you?'

'The daily commute from my place in Brooklyn to work ... Just a sec.'

He turned his attention back to his phone.

'Send. Er ... I teach mentally handicapped kids up in Harlem how to swim.'

A warship was anchored in the Hudson. Jet fighters were lined up on the deck, old models that had reached the maximum number of flight hours.

A brief drum roll burst from the boy's phone. He frowned at his screen.

'Fuck. Gotta take a right here. See you!'

The boy took hold of his handlebars. No record today. He braked, turned, and an eagle swooped towards 42nd Street.

• • • •

I WAS LEVEL WITH MIDTOWN. The traffic on the bike lane thinned out. Were the local business types less inclined to hop on a bike than SoHo's culture vultures?

I'd been too enthusiastic with the saddle and now it was a touch too high. Nothing else for it, I'd have to stop for another fiddle.

Down the street to my right, I recognised the red 'M' on the roof of a tall building: the Milford Plaza Hotel on 45th Street. I had stayed there on my first ever trip to New York in 1980 and been dazzled by the grand scale of it all: a new horizon, different light, different soundscape. After checking in, I had taken the elevator to my room on the 20th floor to discover a view that took in the full length of 8th Avenue. At last, the city of my dreams! I remembered diving headfirst onto the bed, the pillow smothering a primal scream of pure joy.

I stopped by a bench along the Hudson. The wind had kept my head cool while I was on the move but now the sweat was streaming down my temples. I leaned my bike against the back of the bench and took a seat. In the distance I could make out the steel colossus of Washington Bridge, helping the crush of Manhattan traffic across the Hudson to New Jersey. The bridge was my next stop.

I wondered if there was any peace to be had in New York. Behind me was the din of a headlong rush: thundering engines, screeching trucks, taxis rattling with metal fatigue. Not to mention the sirens. The emergency services seemed to be on the go 24/7: a fire here, a heart attack there, the day's umpteenth shooting.

Yet on a flat rock at the river's edge one man seemed suspended in time, arms held out in front of him, hands and fingers extended. Slowly his arms began to sway as his body turned. Tai chi. In the strangest places in Manhattan you could still find people rooted to the spot. Here you had to focus to relax.

A ladies' bike was propped up against the bench next to mine. A relatively small model, just right for a schoolgirl. A man was sitting there, looking out across the water. There was a dullness to the black of his skin. He was wearing baggy sweatpants, cracked Crocs on his bare feet. His fingers were playing with his dreadlocks; frazzled rats' tails sticking out in all directions.

Every inch of the bike's frame was covered in stickers. Stickers promoting brands, sports teams, companies, names I didn't know. Dog-eared stickers, many peeling or torn at the edges. Colourful scabs that had been picked open. Here and there, the frame peeped through: a fetching shade of pink.

I grabbed my mobile phone and pretended to be engrossed in what I saw on the screen. Meanwhile I directed the lens of the built-in camera at the man and his bike. The sun's glare made it tricky to frame the shot. I turned the phone 90 degrees to make a landscape photo and tapped the button on the screen.

A giveaway click.

My unwitting subject heard it too.

'Hey, man, what you think you're doin'?'

Caught red-handed.

'I like your bike.'

Damage limitation. Weasel your way out of it, Wil. I tucked my phone away and walked over to introduce myself. His T-shirt bore the legend MY NAME IS above a white box. In it, a name had been scrawled in marker by a shaky hand: 'Trouble'.

'Stickers is made for stickin',' said the man, without looking at me. Still turning one of his dreadlocks between the fingers of one hand, he extended his other hand towards me. 'Hey, Mister Nice Guy. My name's Trouble. What's yours?'

I told him my name. He hadn't a hope.

'Wolf? Nice.'

Wolf. I'd been called worse in my time. No problem, I could be Wolf for a day.

'What make do you ride?' I asked, pointing at his bike.

'Budweiser, Dodge, Delta, Sneakers, Tamoil, New York Post, Gillette, Diet Coke. Bike of a hundred brands.'

From the shape of the steel frame, I could tell the bike was a few years old. A double tube curved down from the handlebars to the chain guard.

'Saw a squirrel in that tree yesterday,' said Trouble. 'I was sitting right where you're sitting now when I heard him. Snuck down the trunk and ran over to the Hudson for a wash. Some of them waves went clean over his head. I like squirrels.'

Trouble looked at me. He had two mismatched eyes: one stared straight ahead while the other seemed to be asleep, partly hidden under a sagging eyelid.

'Don't believe me, do ya, Wolf?' he said. 'Well then, don't.'

He finished fingering his dreadlocks and felt each one in turn with his palm. 'Need to look my best today. The fumes mess with my hair. Water turns brown when I wash it.'

All at once he lowered his hands.

'You collect stickers too?' he asked, out of the blue.

''Fraid not.'

Trouble stood up, grabbed his bike and set it down in front of me.

'Here, look.'

He was pointing at the seatpost. Next to a chewed-up sticker of the Stars and Stripes was a shiny new silver apple.

59

'Cool. Where did you get that one?' I enquired.

'Courtesy of the doorman at the Apple Store on Prince Street. Fat Jay. Used to go to school together back in Melrose. You heard of Melrose? Over on the other side of the East River.'

From the pocket of his threadbare sweatpants he produced a brown paper bag and shook out a few peanuts. One by one he placed them on the spot where his thumbnail had once been and flipped them into his mouth in a high arc.

'Want some?'

He filled my palm with peanuts.

I tried to ape his technique. At my first attempt, the peanut shot off to the side and rolled under the bench.

'What you do that for?' said Trouble. He sounded disappointed, like a child who had missed out on a treat.

'Sorry, haven't got the hang of it yet,' I answered.

'The crumbs are for the squirrels,' said Trouble. 'I always give 'em something, or they won't survive. See them crows? They're always sneaking in, snatching the peanuts away. Thieving assholes. If I catch 'em, I'll rip their heads off and sell the carcasses to the Chinese down on Canal Street.'

He fell silent and started picking at a sticker with his one remaining thumbnail. The stickers on parts of his bike were several layers thick. A patch of fluorescent yellow caught my eye. On it was a phone number, in the same shaky handwriting as the name on his T-shirt. It began '212'. A New York number.

'Hey, Trouble?'

It was the first time I had used his name. 'Who are you planning to call?' I pointed to the patch of yellow on the frame.

'I don't know you, Wolf. You don't know me. So what's it to you?'

Trouble was right. I didn't know him. I had to work out what made him tick.

'It's just that I like your bike. You know, with all the stickers,' I said.

'Like hell you do, Wolf.'

Trouble got to his feet and grabbed the handlebars with one hand. He clenched his other hand and slammed it down on the saddle.

I jumped and sat bolt upright on the bench.

'You got that?' he said.

Another blow to the saddle.

'I made myself clear?'

He stared at me with a wild look in his eyes.

'I made myself clear, Wolf?' he repeated.

Now that his eyes were wide open I saw how old Trouble really was. Thirty-five was my guess. Till then I'd had him down as late forties, due to the lines on his weary face.

'All right, all right,' I said to calm him.

A man came puffing up the lane on a folding bike with small wheels. Feet spinning way too fast and a hefty paunch under his Chicago Bulls shirt.

'Wrong club, mister!' Trouble shouted after him.

The man played deaf and cycled on his way.

I gazed out at the river. Sailing boats anchored near the wooden breakwaters bobbed about on the Hudson.

'Where you headed?' Trouble shot me a penetrating look.

'Inwood.'

'Heading that way myself. It's my little girl's birthday.'

I took the brownie from my back pocket and carefully peeled the sticker off the cellophane. BAKED JUST FOR YOU, MY PRETTY. I held it out to Trouble.

Without reading the slogan, he stuck it on his headlight.

I unwrapped the brownie and broke it in half. We ate without speaking.

'We goin'?' asked Trouble at last.

'Hang on a sec,' I said, leaning on my saddle with both hands and then tightening the handle.

Trouble took hold of his handlebars and walked unevenly over to the bike lane, as if he had a stone in his shoe. He could ease onto the saddle of his schoolgirl bike without swinging his leg over. 'Let's go.'

For the first few kilometres, we cycled in silence, side by side. I reckoned it would take us another 15 minutes to reach Inwood. What had I got myself into?

Trouble cycled north at a sluggish pace. A familiar figure came cycling towards us. I recognised the shirt: Chicago Bulls.

'Told you already, mister: wrong club!' Trouble bellowed.

The man in the Bulls shirt braked and went to get off his bike.

Trouble slowed down and was clearly intending to stop.

I pulled up alongside him and grabbed his sleeve.

'Leave it, Trouble. A New Yorker's got no time to waste on the Windy City.'

Trouble spat, but no spittle appeared from between his lips. He looked me in the eye but let me drag him on. His right pedal scraped the chain guard at every stroke.

The man in the Bulls shirt glared after us and thrust a middle finger in the air. I thanked my lucky stars that Trouble wasn't looking.

I let go of his sleeve. As we cycled on, Trouble's face clouded over.

'Thing is, Wolf,' he said in a confidential tone, 'I need money.'

I kept quiet, playing for time.

'Money, Wolf,' he said, with the stress on the dosh.

The bike lane stretched on ahead of us. Washington Bridge was coming up on the left. I still had miles to go till my turning point and suddenly my main objective had become making it back to civilisation in one piece. With eight lanes of traffic racing up and down West Street to my right, I had no hope of disappearing into the busy streets of Manhattan. Besides, running scared would be a pitiful end to my first day's cycling in New York. Perhaps I needed to tough this one out.

Trouble was frowning angrily and muttering to himself. He grabbled in his pocket and stuffed a handful of peanuts in his mouth. Half of them fell on the ground.

'Look, you seem like a nice guy, Trouble. But give you money? Why should I? Anyway, I don't have much with me. Just a couple of ten-dollar bills to pay for the bike.'

Trouble grabbed my arm viciously and I tried to fend him off. Our handlebars almost locked.

'Hands off!' I barked.

Trouble took hold of me again, more gently this time.

'My little girl turns 13 today. I want to buy her a little something.'

At Central Station in Amsterdam I had once given 50 euros to a troubled man so that he could catch a train to see his dying father. I believed every word. Till I saw him giving exactly the same spiel to another traveller a week later.

'You don't believe me, do you?' Trouble asked.

'Got that right,' I said.

We were approaching Washington Bridge and I felt myself shrink as the massive steel construction loomed closer. The wind blew the noise of the traffic our way. Row upon row of cars, an endless slow-motion stream.

The bike lane ran under the ramp of the bridge. Traffic thundered over metal ten metres above us. A hellish din.

'Fuck this!' Trouble shouted, spraying peanut crumbs.

He spurted ahead of me and then braked suddenly. My front wheel slammed into his rear mudguard. For the first time I saw a nervous tick twist Trouble's features, as his eyebrows twitched and his eyes blinked and widened.

'Your phone,' he yelled. 'Give me your fuckin' phone!'

I looked around. No one in sight. I decided to negotiate.

'Okay, take my money. But let me keep the phone.'

Trouble threw his bike to the ground and bore down on me. I was standing with the crossbar between my legs. He grabbed my shirt and leaned in close. His skin was like worn black sandpaper.

He stood there motionless, then closed his eyes and heaved a sigh. His shoulders slumped and he loosened his grip.

'Sorry,' I heard him mumble. And then, more softly, 'Sorry, man.'

When he turned, I saw that the whites of his eyes were shot through with red. He looked at me, a broken man.

'Could you get your phone out, Wolf? Please? And call this number for me?'

Trouble picked his bike up off the ground and pointed at the fluorescent sticker on the frame.

'And then what? Who's going to pick up?'

'Just make the call. Please.'

The tension had ebbed away. I decided to make the call.

I fished the phone from my back pocket and tapped in the number. Trouble stood there gawping at me. His eyes flashed open in another nervous tick.

Someone picked up. Soul music blared in the background.

'Hello?'

The bright voice of a young girl amid a flurry of teenage squeals and giggles.

Trouble waved his hands, a sign that I was supposed to say something. But what?

'Hello-o, this is birthday girl Tracy Stanford,' she said with a little laugh. 'Who's calling?'

'Uh, this is, uh … Wolf.'

Trouble moved closer. 'Tell her I'm on my way over.'

'I, uh … Trouble wants me to tell …'

Trouble's hands twitched anxiously. 'Daddy, tell her Daddy.'

'Uh, Daddy says he's on his way,' I said.

'And he's bringing your pink bike,' Trouble prompted. He edged closer still to hear the response at the other end of the line.

'And he's bringing your pink bike,' I repeated.

Not a word. Only Alicia Keys belting out her New York anthem in the background. The giggling had stopped.

'Hello?' I said.

'Tell that motherfucker he ain't Daddy no more.' A dry click. The line went dead.

I could tell from Trouble's face that he'd got the message.

'What did she say?'

'That she doesn't want to see you.'

He shook his head and patted his dreadlocks with one hand.

'Fourth year in a row she don't want me there,' he said.

I slid the phone back in my pocket.

'Where does she live?'

'Somewhere. Okay? With my ex.'

He looked up at the underbelly of the bridge. The traffic had ground to a halt, the cars on the Manhattan-bound lane stood bumper to bumper.

Trouble gave his bike a violent shove.

'What are you doing?' I yelled.

It sped along the bike lane, veered sharp right and clattered to the ground. Trouble charged after it and kicked a hole in the canvas chain guard.

Slowly I cycled over to him and laid my hand on his shoulder.

'Want me to call again?' I asked.

He shoved my hand away and shook his head.

'No, she doesn't want me. Shit. Oh well, tomorrow's another day.'

He picked at the fluorescent sticker and kept on picking till the pink of the frame appeared. He placed the sticky yellow ball on the knuckles of one hand and flicked it away with the other. Then he stooped to pick up his bike.

'I'm going back to my bench,' he said.

I reached for my wallet and pulled out a ten-dollar bill.

'Here,' I said.

Trouble took the bill and kissed it.

'Thank you, Mister Nice Guy.' He waved the bill in front of my nose and stuffed it in his pocket. 'That'll get me a new bag of peanuts.'

He cycled off at a sluggish pace.

I passed under the bridge and continued my journey along the bike lane. It led to a narrow bridge for cyclists that spanned the busy traffic on West Street. From there I was able to cut through to Inwood. Once I got there, I cycled straight ahead for a few blocks till I hit Broadway. I took a right and began my southward leg. The famous avenue ran from the Bronx deep into Manhattan, the life-line on a creased old palm.

No hope of a smooth ride. At every junction it was a toss-up whether I would make the lights in time. In fits and starts I reached Harlem, took Lenox Avenue and headed for Central Park. A woman in a wheelchair was sitting outside a hospital entrance with a blue cap over her mouth to protect her from the exhaust fumes.

Fresh air didn't come for free up in Harlem either.

My journey ended at the bollards that marked the start of Times Square. I got off the bike and took a look around. On a giant screen, luscious lips five metres wide pouted for a lipstick the size of an Exocet missile.

Was Trouble already back on his bench, looking out across the Hudson?

• • •

BACK AT THE HOTEL, my quilt had been turned down and a brownie wrapped in cellophane graced my pillow. Light brown this time. On the bottom it read: THIS BABY IS A NATURAL BLONDE.

I ripped open the blonde's cellophane wrapper and bit into her soft middle. She was gone in three bites. No crumbs for the squirrels.

I undressed and slid my weary legs between the sheets.

On the TV screen, NYPD's finest were out on a raid, ramming down a door as a cameraman breathed down their necks. In no time a huddle of startled young men were being cuffed and bundled into a waiting van. They swore to the police officers that they were going to mend their ways. Starting tomorrow. I could tell they were lying.

Tomorrow is another day.

WOOL

New York

RED LIGHT. A bike messenger pulled up next to me, slid his sunglasses high on his forehead and wiped a gloved hand across his brow.

'Busy day?' I asked.

'Busy as hell,' the young man said, tightening the buckle on the bag strapped to his back.

The light seemed to be stuck on red. Behind us, a slot-machine jackpot of three yellow cabs was lined up, raring to go.

I had just pumped up my tyres at a nearby garage and leaned forwards to check the pressure. The courier watched me press my thumb into the profile of my front wheel. Rock hard, to see me through the evening with a minimum of friction.

'High pressure, man,' he said.

'Yeah,' I said, trying way too hard to sound hip. 'High pressure for the high priest of bop.'

I took secret pleasure in the frown that creased his forehead. How could I explain the euphoria that had taken hold of me since my plane had landed at JFK? Impossible. On my last visit to New York I'd been lumbered with a clunky rental bike and a ladies' saddle. This time I was taking no chances: my extra baggage consisted of my very own racing bike. Custom-made and named after the high priest of jazz pianists, a man who had lived and breathed this city. I would be riding the streets of New York on Thelonious. My own personal tribute to Thelonious Monk.

Green at last!

The courier let his sunglasses slide down onto the bridge of his nose and shot off on his worn-out fixed gear. Off on the next stage of his day-long race through the ultimate urban grid.

The sky above the skyscrapers of 6th Avenue glowed deep purple. Magic over Manhattan. Thelonious and I skirted two double-parked trucks and were soon up to a decent tempo, despite checking and weaving our way through the flow of traffic.

Another red light. I braked. To save unclipping my shoes, I leaned against the roof of a waiting taxi. Level with the passenger door, I peered in at the back-seat customer, lost in the front page of the *Wall Street Journal*. The hands on his chunky wristwatch told me it was three minutes past nine.

* * *

THE TRAFFIC GRADUALLY EASED INTO MOTION AGAIN. I pedalled to the rhythm of 'Monk's Mood', a ballad in a minor key that had been moping around my head for weeks. Charlie Rouse's introverted tenor sax sobbed sweetly in the middle register, feeling its way towards a foothold in the chord changes.

My first stop was Greenwich Village, a good neighbourhood for tracking down second-hand jazz albums. What better way to round off my first evening in New York than by riding back to my SoHo hotel with a collector's item tucked under my arm?

I turned into a narrow side street off Bleecker and had to swerve as a car door was flung open. A woman carrying a lampshade stepped out into the street without a care in the world. I cycled on. Out of the corner of my eye, I spotted a bunch of LP covers hanging in a dingy shop window. I hopped onto the sidewalk and parked my bike in front of the store.

Jazz! I hadn't been mistaken. Nose almost pressed to the window pane, I inspected the covers. An original Prestige by saxophonist Willis Jackson, a first pressing by the look of it. *Testifyin' Time* by Bunky Green on the Argo label. Not in the best of nick, if the ragged edges of the cover were anything to go by. Oscar Peterson, not really my bag. Oscar's pudgy fingers might move at ten times the speed of Monk's, but my high priest outdid him every time with his stirring, stabbing transitions from white keys to black.

The store owner came outside with a pile of LPs. The top one had an orange SALE sticker slapped on it. He slid the records into a box beside the door.

We looked at each other and he gave me a friendly nod, before turning his attention to my bike.

'Wow, nice frame.'

'Thanks.'

The man had a tangle of curly hair and a long goatee. A black bead dangled at the end like a stray punctuation mark.

'What make is it?'

I pointed at the light-grey letters on the seat tube. The owner crouched to take a closer look and read the name aloud.

'Pay-go-ready!' He might have been auditioning for Scorsese's latest gangster epos.

'Pegoretti,' I replied, in my juiciest Italian.

My fingers slid across the thin black lines that covered the frame and always reminded me of music staves.

'The bike's a tribute to Thelonious Monk. Pegoretti always paints his frames personally.'

The man nodded. '"Blue Monk", man, "Blue Monk"!' He began whistling the melody. An apparently simple blues, constructed from an ascending ladder of clear notes.

He twisted the bead at the end of his goatee and continued to gaze at the frame in fascination.

'How 'bout a cup of tea?' he asked, looking up at me. Pale eyes in a pasty face.

'I'd love to. But I don't have a lock for my bike.'

His nicotine fingers let the bead fall and he gestured to me. 'No problem. Take Thelonious inside. Straight through, down three stairs and keep going till you reach the end. You'll see my wheels back there too.'

I lifted my bike across the threshold and squeezed through the narrow aisle that ran down the middle of the shop, hemmed in by wooden racks packed with LPs. I breathed in the penetrating smell of patchouli, signature scent of the trippy sixties.

'Campagnolo forever,' the store owner called after me.

He must know his bikes or he'd never have recognised the sound of my rear mech. I went down the steps and laid eyes on his bike, or rather the contours of his bike. The entire frame was covered in wool. Every tube was wrapped in the stuff. Even the wheels had been woven solid. Not a spoke to be seen. It was as if a psychedelic spider had taken possession of the thing. A finely woven web was stretched across the triangle of the frame.

'My own little Bianchi,' said the owner fondly.

I would never have recognised the classic Italian make through its disguise.

'Answers to the name of Loulou.'

'Cool,' I lied. A steel frame is a manly thing. There was something perverse about a woolly bike. Too soft, too comfy. What had he been thinking?

I leaned the steel of Thelonious against Loulou's fuzzy frame. Quite the couple. To have and to hold from this day forth.

The owner had wandered back into his store. I followed him through and saw him standing at an improvised cupboard kitchenette. He placed an old singing kettle on the hob and lit the gas.

I strolled past the record racks. Gene Ammons was leaning against Art Blakey, who in turn was nudging the belly of John Coltrane. ABC. Then came Miles under D, up close and personal with Duke Ellington, followed by the Chicago tenors Von Freeman and Johnny Griffin.

The kettle wailed and the owner poured boiling water over bunches of mint sticking out of two mugs. From a square box with Chinese characters he produced two tiny black balls and tossed them in too.

Not your average cuppa.

He handed me a mug and walked over to a rack of new arrivals. His fingers flicked expertly through the huddle of LP covers. He pulled one out, coaxed the vinyl from its sleeve and placed it carefully on the turntable. He bent over, blew on the needle and swung the arm over the disc. The needle descended slowly into its groove.

A techno beat and a spot of heavy breathing. It took me a second or two to catch on.

'Kraftwerk. "Tour de France",' I grinned.

'Right first time. From 1983. Back when I was ten.'

Kraftwerk. I could still recall the visuals. Four men on bikes, speeding past like an express train.

We slurped our tea in the deserted shop. The owner painstakingly pushed his mint leaves down into his mug.

'Do you and ... er ... Loulou get around much?'

'Nah, mostly just to the store and back.'

I tried to spit a few bitter black leaves into my mug without him noticing. I had a couple of mouth ulcers on the inside of my lip and I was beginning to have my doubts about this brew of his.

'It was my mother who covered my bike in wool. My parents moved to East Harlem in 1987, a big apartment near Jefferson Park. After my dad died, she couldn't sleep alone. So now I live there too. More tea?'

'I'll pass, thanks.'

Beside my mug, I spotted a pile of business cards in the form of a record. PHIL'S PLACE. SECONDHAND RECORDS, OLDIES BUT GOODIES.

I picked one up.

'So you're Phil?' I asked.

'Phil, yeah. Rhymes with over the hill.'

From the racks of jazz LPs, I pulled out an old Riverside album. Monk with Mulligan on baritone sax. I teased the inner sleeve out of the thick cardboard cover. The smell of a newspaper archive rose up, paper with a lifetime of service behind it. I placed the dull vinyl on one of the turntables, slipped on a pair of headphones and cranked up the volume.

A frantic outburst. The fanatical hammering of piano keys. It conjured up visions of the Monk I knew from the documentary *Straight, No Chaser*. Letting off steam in front of a live audience. Satin hat and long black coat. He looked like a black Orthodox Jew in the throes of a mystic seizure. His solo done, he rose to his feet and began to spin manically, blindly. Whirling in a trance, caught up in the undercurrent of his music. Incomplete, searching, awash with furious swing. Eyes tight shut, hurtling through a dissonant universe. An odyssey reserved for Monk and Monk alone.

Wild chords stopped abruptly as the headphones were pulled from my ears. I turned and looked into Phil's grinning face.

'It'll make you deaf, up that loud.'

'With Monk, it can never be loud enough.'

Phil pulled a 45 from another rack. A picture sleeve of a wild man in a glitter cape and star-shaped sunglasses. Gazing out at the world imperiously from over his keyboards.

'Sun Ra,' said Phil. 'Wait till you hear this.'

He put the single on the turntable and nudged up the volume. The speakers hanging from the ceiling crackled into life before blaring a cacophony of messy jazz and atonal electronics. Phil stood in the middle of his store, head bobbing, eyes closed.

Sun Ra was quite a guy. He lived in a commune with his musicians and saw the Earth as an insignificant speck in the cosmos. His music was a spiritual quest, a way to tune into the Milky Way. Jupiter was a favourite planet of his, a wild and wonderful place to be. Life here on Earth just wasn't inspiring enough for Ra.

'Space is the place!' Phil sang along. 'Space is the place.'

It was a few minutes before he opened his eyes again. He looked at me, dazed, lifted the needle from the vinyl and toddled over to his kitchenette.

'Nice, eh? It's yours. I'll set it aside for you.' He tucked the single back into its sleeve.

'Too kind,' I said.

Monk was still spinning. I hung the headphones on their hook. Mulligan's sax sounded soft and nasal through the tiny speakers.

Phil put a fresh mug of tea on the counter for me. I didn't have the heart to refuse a second time. Had it never dawned on anyone to collect those noxious leaves in a teabag and attach a string?

'On vacation?' Phil looked at me and held his mug to his lips for a long time before taking a sip. A little piece of mint stuck to his teeth.

'Yeah, five days. Sounds mad, but I wanted to break in my bike somewhere special. And New York's the ideal playground for Thelonious.'

Phil stood up and marched outside. Through the dirty window I saw him lift the box of records from the sidewalk and carry it back inside. 'Time to call it a day!' he exclaimed. 'Closed for business.'

I looked up at the clock above the cash register. Five to ten. It was dark outside.

'No need to rush. Spin another record. Pull the plug on the headset and the music will come through the speakers, loud and clear.'

I returned to the Monk rack and found a Riverside LP from 1958, in decent condition to boot. *At the Five Spot.* One of the best Monk sets ever to be committed to vinyl, live from a Manhattan jazz club. The inner sleeve was original and almost crackled to the touch. I could read the titles on the blue label through the translucent paper. 'Light Blue', 'Coming on the Hudson', 'Rhythm-A-Ning'.

Phil released a cord next to the door and a roller blind thundered down. Shielded from the streetlights, the store was almost plunged into darkness. The only light came from a table lamp on the counter and a bare bulb hanging above the bikes through the back.

I pulled the plug on the headphones and Monk came shining through in all his glory. For the first few bars of his solo he seemed to be half-blind, feeling his way, working out the breadth of the path. Then, realising there was nothing in the chord scheme to hold him back, he took off, spiralling in all directions. Notes tumbled from the speakers, pure and open.

Monk unleashed.

Phil totted up the day's takings. Glancing over, I saw no more than a couple of bills disappear into his back pocket. Business wasn't exactly booming. Each turn of the Riverside LP was accompanied by a vicious click. Shame. But for that I would have bought it.

Monk launched into the second tune of his set. Was this record an ode to Pannonica de Koenigswarter, New York's own jazz baroness, with a predilection for stray cats and stray musicians?

Both had regularly found refuge in her apartment overlooking the Hudson. Pannonica took Monk under her wing towards the end, cared for the reclusive pianist like a son. No more worries about a bed for the night or where his next meal was coming from, and if a jazz club was within driving distance, his guardian angel would chauffeur him there in her clapped-out old Bentley.

Phil had settled down on an old couch opposite Loulou and Thelonious, and lit up a joint. Grey strands of smoke wound around the light bulb. The feeble light shone down from above and made him look weary.

He took a long drag on his joint and held in the smoke for a long time before exhaling. After another deep inhalation, he stretched out on the couch. I looked down at the spinning vinyl and watched the needle glide smoothly over the grooves of the final tune, tapping along with the tight rhythm of the cymbals.

In the back room, Phil was upright again. He reached out and grabbed the handlebars of my bike, squeezed the brake and watched the brake pads make contact with the rim of the front wheel. He squeezed again, puffing away at his joint all the while.

Call me old-fashioned, but I don't like strange men fooling around with my bike. Thelonious was made to measure. We were perfectly attuned, he and I. Something had to be said. I walked over to the couch just as Phil was stubbing out his joint in a glass ashtray. He looked up at me. The white of his eyes had turned red.

'In the fall I want to go on a real long bike trip. New York to Frisco. Travellin' light. Two small saddlebags, a sleeping bag and a few bits and pieces. Take my mandolin and enough money to get by and just see where I end up. I've never been out on the open road. My parents hardly ever left the city. A day out in Upstate New York at most. Dad always wanted to be close to his work and Mom didn't like sleeping in a strange bed. She's afraid of the dark. That's why I moved in with her. She's always worrying about me, always wants to know where I am. Rattling around that big apartment all alone scares her.'

Out of nowhere, Phil began to sob. His shoulders shook. He mumbled an apology and headed for the toilet. The green of the latch turned red.

Monk had returned to the main theme of his last tune. The piano sounded muffled. Dust on the needle? I sat down on the couch opposite Thelonious and Loulou and looked at the wool on the bike. How much time and effort it must have taken to wrap every inch of every tube in strands of different colours. The wheels were woven solid and almost looked like the disc wheels that pros use in time trials. I tried to picture the likes of Cancellara and Wiggins powering through the prologue of the Tour de France on woolly wheels.

Phil emerged from the toilet and sat down next to me. He blew his nose on a few sheets of toilet paper, scrunched them up and held them in his cupped hand.

'Sorry about that. It's not easy for me to talk about Mom.'

'No problem. Must be tough looking after your mother like that.'

'Yeah, can be.'

He dabbed one nostril with the scrunched-up tissue.

'More tea?' he asked.

'Er, no, I've had enough. Really.'

Monk played his final chord, holding down the keys so the higher tones continued to resonate. Then the crackle of the final groove took over, followed by a click as the arm lifted and the turntable shut itself down.

I hadn't come all the way to New York to hang around on a threadbare couch in the back room of a record store. I was itching to whizz up and down the asphalt of those world-famous avenues.

'You said you and your mother live in East Harlem?' I asked. 'A few years back I went to Smoke, that jazz place on the corner of Broadway and 106th Street. It's not far from you.'

Phil gave a few tugs on his goatee, popped the black bead in his mouth and shook his head.

'Smoke, you say? No, don't know it.'

'Tonight it's piano. Harold Mabern is playing three sets. It's coming up for 11. We might just make the second one.'

I saw him thinking.

'Don't worry. We won't stay out all night.'

'Sounds good,' he said at last. He walked up to me and patted my shoulder. 'In that case, count me in.'

Phil extinguished his joint under the cold tap. He pulled a woollen hat from a basket beside the cash register and stuck it on his head. He handed me the Sun Ra single. 'Don't forget this.'

I thanked him and stuck the 45 under my jersey. The braces of my cycling shorts would hold it in place.

Phil flicked the main switch. In the dark, I felt my way to Thelonious, he to Loulou. We left by the back door. Out on the street, Phil strapped a light to his arm. I had nothing with me, road sense stymied by the thrill of being here.

Phil clambered onto Loulou, slid his hand back and forth along the handlebars, tapped three times on the woollen web of his front wheel and made a sign of the cross.

Off we went.

The asphalt was holding on to the heat of the day, but the wind had turned colder. Phil led the way and I saw passers-by turn their heads to take a second look. Even for a jaded New Yorker, a woolly bike was a sight to behold.

His route made no sense to me. We turned down one side street then another, occasionally getting off and walking a stretch of sidewalk. Things only became clearer as we headed north along Central Park. I drew level with Phil and looked at him. With his long goatee swaying in the breeze he could have come straight out of Tolkien. *Lord of the Rings* live on Broadway.

We reached 110th Street and skirted the northern edge of Central Park. From the Broadway intersection it was only a few blocks south to 106th Street. We had left the skyscrapers behind us. This section of Manhattan was more apartments than offices. Even at this late hour, plenty of shops and cafés were still open for business.

Up ahead I spotted the sign for Smoke.

'Here it is,' I shouted to Phil.

We dismounted, wheeled our bikes onto the sidewalk and looked for a good spot to park. The entrance to Smoke was guarded by a tall black doorman with a friendly face and sporting a baseball cap.

"Scuse me, sir, we're here to see the show. Is there anywhere safe to leave our bikes?'

The doorman's laugh was deep and warm. 'You're on racing bikes? Sorry, guys. The show's for businessmen and Japanese tourists. Suited and booted.'

I looked down. Bare from the knee, white sports socks, silver cycling shoes. Beside me stood a latter-day beatnik in a crumpled T-shirt with a black bead dangling from his goatee and a bike covered in wool. I could see where the doorman was coming from. After all, he was paid to keep out the freaks.

'Where you from? Outer space?'

The doorman chuckled mightily and stamped his foot to underline the hilarity of it all.

Phil looked devastated. I could see he wasn't going to be much help but the doorman's space jibe had triggered something. In a last-ditch attempt to prove our jazz credentials, I pulled the Sun Ra 45 from under my shirt and flashed him the cover. 'Outer space. Spot on, man. Disciples of Ra since the dawn of time.'

At the sound of Ra's name, Phil came to life and began to hum the tune he'd been blaring along to back at the shop.

'Space is the place!' The doorman not only joined in but stepped out onto the sidewalk, raised his hands to heaven like a gospel preacher and gyrated his hips. His moves rang a bell; I remembered Sun Ra doing that very dance when he and his Arkestra played a late-night session at the Jazzbunker in Rotterdam.

I tucked the single back under my shirt and gave him a round of applause.

We had won him over. I could feel it in my bones.

'You guys know Sun Ra? Then you're one of the club. 'Scuse me a second.'

He walked over to a taxi and opened the back door. An Asian man emerged, followed by a leggy beauty in stilettos. She was head and shoulders above him in more ways than one.

'Welcome to Smoke, Mr Hiu-Kee, sir.'

The doorman gave a slight bow and proceeded to escort them to the entrance. The man slipped him a tip and he and his lady friend disappeared inside. The doorman turned back to us.

'Sun Ra! Unbelievable! Listen, guys, I'd like to help you with the bikes but this is a small club and we're packing 'em in tonight.'

I looked around and spotted a lamppost some ten metres down the street. Too far from the door for my liking but needs must.

'Tell you what, we'll chain our bikes to that lamppost, as long as we can take our front wheels in with us. No thief's going to run off with a bike that's missing a wheel.'

Phil nodded.

'Could you keep an eye out?' I asked the doorman.

'Even if they fly off into the cosmos, I'll be right behind 'em,' he laughed.

I might have known: even Phil's lock was sheathed in wool. Within minutes Thelonious and Loulou were shackled to the lamppost. Front wheels in hand, we strolled back over to the doorman. Shaking his head in disbelief, he tore us off two tickets.

'This one's on me,' I told Phil. 'It's the least I can do after the gift of Ra.'

Phil gave a shy, broad grin. In we went, wheels and all.

A girl yelled in my ear. 'Table or bar, Mr Biker, sir?'

'Bar,' I yelled back.

The set was already in full swing and the place was heaving. The waitress directed us to two stools over by the toilets at the side of the small stage and handed us the drinks menu. I ordered two beers. Large ones.

As I was taking my first sip, I glanced over to see Phil draining his glass, beer dribbling down his chin. He put down his glass, wiped his goatee and sucked on the bead at the end.

Harold Mabern was at the piano heading up a tight trio. I had first seen him live at B14 in Rotterdam back in the late 1970s, playing with a quartet led by alto sax player Frank Strozier. I had always remembered his hands, the size of coal shovels. Here I was again, spellbound as he pawed at the keys.

Phil ordered two more beers from the barman.

I looked down at the front wheel clamped between his knees. The dedication behind the intricate patterns in the wool was a marvel. The same motif recurred at four different points on the wheel: a shield, still colourful, though faded by the sun. It reminded me of a heraldic coat of arms.

I nudged Phil and pointed at the pattern.

'Yeah, cool aren't they? Mom came up with them. I don't know what they mean. Some shit from way back.'

The drummer got stuck into his solo and we had to raise our voices to be heard.

'Your old lady's a true artist.'

'Thanks. Yeah, nothing she can't do with a ball of wool. Never throws anything away. Born out in the sticks, among the sheep and the cows.'

'How long did it take her to do the wheel?'

'Er ... a week tops, I think. Wow, this guy can really drum. What's his name?'

'Joe Farnsworth.'

Farnsworth produced some dazzling brushwork on the snare drum. The crowd urged him on to new heights, faster, more furious.

'Go for it, man!' Phil shouted. The beer had loosened him up at bit.

I imagined him going home to his mother in a while, slightly the worse for wear, tucking her in and stroking her thinning hair.

'No mean feat, looking after your mom day in, day out. Don't you ever feel like striking out on your own?'

I had hit a nerve. Phil turned to me and his tone turned steely. 'When somebody's taken care of you their whole life, you gotta do what you can when they get old. But I don't want to talk about it. She ain't here and it feels like a betrayal. You understand?'

Without replying, I took a gulp of beer. This was a rare night out for him. I should never have started on about his mother. Phil turned his attention to the stage, where bass and piano had joined the drums once again. He drank it all in, eyes flashing to and fro. As an encore, the trio launched into a reinvention of Stevie Wonder's 'Sir Duke'. The whole place clapped along, all except Phil.

When the applause died away, the bassist and the drummer headed straight for the bar. Harold Mabern lingered at the piano, chatting to a Japanese fan who had been taking photos throughout the show. He signed a copy of his latest CD. Online I had read that Mabern was Smoke's pianist in residence. The man was probably in his late seventies. He had played with Miles Davis, Wes Montgomery and Lionel Hampton.

Mabern drained a glass of water and wandered over to the bar. He looked us up and down, and raised his eyebrows when he caught sight of the woollen wheel clamped between Phil's knees.

'You play the psychedelic harp or something?'

Phil laughed shyly. 'Nah, our bikes are parked outside and we reckoned no thief would waste his time on a one-wheeled bike.'

Mabern grabbed the wheel from between Phil's knees.

'Are you nuts?' he exclaimed as his outsized fingers glided across the woollen strands.

I leapt to Phil's defence. 'All done by hand. His mother's work.'

Mabern pointed at my wheel.

'And what about yours?'

I held it by the axis and gave it a spin. 'Mavic Cosmic Carbone. Smooth action, don't you think?'

Mabern looked deadly serious as he followed the spinning of the wheel.

'And where's the rest?' he asked.

'Chained to a lamppost down the street,' I replied.

'His frame's named for Monk,' said Phil.

Mabern nodded in admiration. 'My friend Thelonious, high priest of bop. Nuff said.'

The Japanese fan tapped Mabern's shoulder. 'One more photo, sir?'

The barman handed me the bill. Time to settle up. A new set would soon be under way for a fresh batch of paying customers. I looked up at the clock. 'What time did you want to get home, Phil?'

'Round midnight.'

'Shit, it's already half past. Let's go.'

I tossed two 20-dollar bills on the bar and told the barman he could keep the change. Wheels above our heads, we squeezed through the crowd and out into the night air. The doorman made some space for us and treated us to a reprise of his Sun Ra routine.

'You're in luck. Bikes just got back from Mars.' His belly laugh could be heard above the traffic.

I handed him a five-dollar bill.

Phil unchained our bikes. We reattached our front wheels and Thelonious and Loulou were ready to roll once more.

'Where's your hotel?' he asked.

'SoHo.'

'I'm heading east. We can cycle together for a while. On the corner of Jefferson Park you can head downtown on 1st Avenue. Good bike lane.'

He pulled his light from his pocket and Velcroed it around his arm. We said goodbye to the doorman and turned onto Broadway.

'Stay on my right,' said Phil. 'It's safer that way. They're more likely to see me.'

We cycled back to 110th Street and took a right. A bunch of young skateboarders were honing their skills on a group of park benches.

Four blocks down, someone had traded 110th Street's number for a name: Tito Puente's Boulevard. Had a nice ring to it. Tito Puente: King of the Timbales, a son of Spanish Harlem.

'You into Latin, Phil?'

'Nah, I'm more of a free-jazz guy, sixties and seventies stuff. And I collect everything by Ravi Shankar.'

I knew the name. Indian. Endless albums of whining sitar.

Phil was riding at quite a pace. His thin mudguards were rattling, despite being muffled by the wool. He switched up a few gears and fairly shot along.

'Does your mom always stay up till you get home?' I asked.

No reply.

We took a left and then a right. Jefferson Park came into view, its trees like dark clouds tethered to trunks. Phil braked suddenly. I sailed a few metres past him and ground to a halt.

'1st Avenue. This is where you head right.'

'Thanks, man.'

Phil gave me an awkward slap on the shoulder. I returned the gesture.

'Here, take my light. I've got a spare at home. Might save you some hassle with the cops.'

He pulled the Velcro loose and the red glow illuminated his face, turning him into a goateed albino. 'Have a nice stay,' he shouted over his shoulder.

From here it was an easy ride back to the hotel: a few kilometres heading directly downtown. Strapping the light to my arm, I watched Phil go. He didn't look back. I saw him riding in the beam of a street lamp, 50 metres or so away. A man and his woolly bike.

I found myself lingering, both feet still firmly on the ground, unable to shake my curiosity about where Phil and his mother lived. I switched off the light on my arm and set off after him. To make sure he wouldn't notice me in the dark, I downshifted and lagged a good 100 metres behind. Smoothly and soundlessly, I began to tail him.

Phil took a right and disappeared from view. I got up on my pedals to reach the junction as quickly as possible, determined not to lose touch.

No one in sight. Shit! Lost him already. As far as I could see, there was no side street he could have cut down. I reduced speed, looking left and right, scanning all the house fronts. Grand buildings with monumental doorways.

To the right I thought I heard a door slam. Phil? I was just about to track down the noise when I caught a glimpse of him in the light of a nearby hallway. He wheeled his bike into the lift and turned around. I ducked out of sight behind a car and hoped he hadn't seen me.

It was more foyer than hallway. Lots of marble and thick pillars decorated with gold paint. A night porter was sitting behind a desk, reading a newspaper by the light of an old-fashioned scissor lamp.

I took a few steps back and looked up to see a third-floor light come on. Instead of curtains hanging either side, a single drape hung in the lighted window, sweeping in from the sides and gathered in the middle. It looked like wool and I could just make out a coat of arms, similar to the one I had seen on Phil's wheels. The light went out after a few minutes. I waited but there was no more sign of Phil or his mother.

I walked my bike up to the doorway and to my surprise the glass doors slid open automatically. Just as I was wondering whether a total stranger with a bike would be welcome, the doorman waved me in.

'Hello, sir, can I help you?'

I hadn't come up with a pretext, but on an impulse I unfastened the light around my arm and showed it to the doorman.

'Phil was kind enough to lend this to me. Could you return it, when you see him?'

'Of course, sir. He's just come in. Would you like me to buzz him?'

'No, thanks. I wouldn't want to disturb his mother.'

'His mother?'

'Yes. He lives with his mother, doesn't he?'

'I'm sorry to be the one to break it to you, sir, but Phil's mother died some years ago.'

My mind began to race as the doorman continued.

'She lived here for 30 years. With her husband. He was a businessman, sold weaving looms all over the world. After he passed away, she never left the house again. Phil had to do everything for her. One evening she walked right past my desk here, dressed to the nines, a woollen hat on her head. Two days later they found her body in the East River.'

We were silent for a moment.

'How do you know Phil, sir? If you don't mind me asking?'

I told him about our meeting at the record store.

'And the two of you went out this evening?'

I nodded.

'Then he must've had the time of his life. I've never known Phil to go out of an evening.'

I laid the light on the desk in front of the doorman.

'Please tell him I said hello.'

'What name should I give, sir?'

'Thelonious.'

'The-lo-ni-ous,' he drawled, writing the name slowly in the margin of his newspaper. 'All right, see you.'

I gave him a friendly nod and wheeled my bike back outside. From the pavement, I took another look up at the apartment. Still no light. All I could see was the vague outline of the drape; the wool hanging down from the middle reminded me of Phil's goatee.

A few powerful strokes on my pedals and I was soon up to speed, making decent headway on the 1st Avenue bike lane. Storefront sales pitches blurred as I whizzed past. I dipped low over the handlebars to catch as little wind as possible and felt Sun Ra prick my skin.

Next stop SoHo.

By the time I reached Prince Street, the melancholy thread of 'Monk's Mood' had woven its way back into my brain: stray notes searching for their place on the staves. I pedalled hard to beat the lights. The black lines of the staves began to ripple. The notes peeled away and flew off across the avenue, searching in vain for a place to call home.

MUNKZWALM

Belgium

THERE ARE PLACE names you don't forget in a hurry. Munkzwalm is surely one. Not a town, not a village, not even a hamlet. No, Munkzwalm. An asphalt-smothered stretch of Flemish clay. One house to the left, one house to the right, a butcher's, a baker's and – let's not talk the place down – one more house for good measure. At a bend in the road, a statue of the Virgin Mary weeps rusty tears of utter desolation. Even the trees around insignificant Munkzwalm hang their heads in shame. The green leaves of spring know the score and hang back in the bud.

I park my car there on a Sunday in April, beside a building that stands alone and goes by the name of Café Taxi. Still over an hour to go before the Tour of Flanders passes this way. I step inside. It's around noon. The pub is heaving. The landlady, five feet two and clad in an apron that reaches the floor, is pulling half-pints like there's no tomorrow. On the sacred days of cycling, the Dutch tourists do their best to be Belgian, complete with local banter and cod Flemish accent. It's marginally less embarrassing than a bunch of Brits heading over to Ireland 'just for the craic, to be sure, to be sure'.

The pub might be called Taxi but no one here is going anywhere. Everyone's staying put. Waiting. Lingering. The television cackles. The Tour is approaching. The race proper has yet to unfold. The peloton make sure their jackets are zipped tight. The riders' thoughts are already turning to the cobbles of the Molen-berg, the first climb of the day. The locals liken those cobbles to children's skulls.

Out beyond the pub's net curtains, the course lies waiting, un-sullied, innocent as yet. I look through the window and see the backs of the spectators lined up along the route. Raincoats. Long, short, beige, brown, black, grubby, freshly pressed. A split up the back for the ladies, handy pockets for the gents.

Every head poking out of a raincoat collar is inclined to the left. As if Munkzwalm has fallen prey to an acute neck-cramp epidemic.

I look at the clock. If it keeps good time – and why should the Café Taxi clock not keep good time? – the riders will pass through Munkzwalm in one hour.

One hour. Just one hour to go. Only 60 minutes before the Tour passes this way.

More and more customers desert the pub and make their way to the roadside. The television shows pictures of the peloton, riders still tightly packed together. I recognise shirts, identify the odd face under a helmet.

The pub becomes emptier and emptier. The landlady gives me a wink and puts another glass of beer down in front of me. Another few minutes and it'll be just the two of us. She walks through a swing door into a back room. Most likely she lives on the premises. The prospect of diving into bed and snuggling up against her warm haunches is enticing. But hang on, the riders are on their way, sweeping all before them. Only 45 minutes to go. The erotic charms of Munkzwalm and Café Taxi are not some-thing you succumb to on a Tour day.

I pay the landlady and walk quickly outside. In a winter coat that's a tad too trendy I take my place among the people. It's cold. Damp cold. Cycling cold. During the Tour of Flanders in April, don't expect any warmth from the clay beneath you. The men around me stamp their feet. Beside me, a woman with a cycling cap on her head removes a boiled sausage from a plastic bag and begins to gnaw on it manically. A little further along, people are clustered three rows deep around a little guy with a transistor radio. The commentator's voice blares hysterically through the speaker.

Once a year, Munkzwalm has a place in the world. Once a year it has cause for celebration. Once a year Munkzwalm appears on TV. World fame for Munkzwalm, kilometre 128 of the Tour of Flanders.

Waiting for riders is an art. Unless you've stood at the side of the road during the Tour, you don't know what the Tour is.

· · ·

HERE COMES THE HELICOPTER. The sound of the rotor blades catapults Munkzwalm into a state of war. Yellow flags bearing lions are thrust into the air like bayonets, banners proclaim love for a cycling hero. The people of Munkzwalm fling themselves like cannon fodder onto the asphalt. The lenses of their cameras are trained on the distance. That's the place. Surely, any moment now, the lads will appear.

A single camera leers in our direction. The man nods. Clicks. Let him get on with it. Right now, we cycling folk are too busy craning our necks.

The helicopter is hanging above our heads. A woman with a child waves up to the family watching at home. Motorcycles tear past, sirens wailing.

And here they come, the riders. Like a vast chameleon the peloton continually changes shape and colour. Four hundred tyres sing to us. Music for a Sunday afternoon.

Here they come.

Here they are.

There they go.

It's all over, consigned to the past once more.

This was Munkzwalm. We can still see the mud-spattered back-side of a straggler, sitting crooked on his bike after a fall. The skin of his elbow has been grazed raw, the dirt of the Tour ground into the wound. But he must go on. The Tour waits for no man.

Café Taxi floods full to bursting.

The mother with child asks if they were on camera. The land-lady saw no one she recognised on TV. Not even her pub. Same story as last year.

We get back to the business of drinking. We eat. We warm our-selves. It feels fine but we know something is missing. TV is a sur-rogate: it shows you everything and that's a bore. It's naked flesh without the lingerie. Not seeing everything is at least as satisfying. We, the true believers, would rather imagine our own Tour.

My second glass is empty. I slip the landlady a farewell wink. 'See you next year,' I lie. She shoots me a gap-toothed grin. I drive my car over the course. The spot where we stood is deserted.

The Virgin Mary has dried her tears. It's an anonymous land-scape: clay, asphalt, here a house, there a house. Slowly Munk-zwalm goes back to being Munkzwalm.

MERCKX TO THE MILLIMETRE

Northern France

ONE BY ONE, cogs, screws, spokes, even the links in the chain are subjected to a final inspection. Time and again, the mechanic's greased fingers glide from one end of the bike to the other. Stroking, massaging, pressing, tickling.

The bicycle as a woman, demanding tender loving care.

The year is 1976, the eve of the Paris–Roubaix cycling classic. The Molteni team is lodging at a hotel close to Chantilly. In a nondescript room, the mechanic is hard at work on the bike of the team's star rider. Everything has been fine-tuned for the bone-shaking ride over the cobbles. His work is done. Or so he thinks.

* * *

EDDY MERCKX DROPS IN. In pidgin Italian he starts spouting numbers, discussing the ideal sitting position. He talks centimetres. No, millimetres.

The mechanic picks up a tape measure and checks the height of the saddle in relation to the orange-brown frame. Every last detail has been meticulously tweaked in proportion to Eddy's physique. The line of his back. The extension of his tendons and muscles as the pedals turn. The jolts to his neck that will be inflicted by ten stretches of notorious cobbles. Eddy is about to enter the Hell of the North and everyone is expecting him to emerge victorious. Doesn't he always? And so the saddle has to be just right.

Merckx sits down on a bench opposite and squints at his bike with dark carpenter's eyes.

The mechanic picks up a retractable ruler, holds one end against the stem and presses the lip at the other end tightly against the back of the saddle. He fiddles beneath the saddle for a moment and then briefly mounts the great man's bike himself. Yes, this is exactly the right setting.

Merckx concedes. His bike is ready to ride.

* * *

JUST BEFORE THE TEAM sets out on the winding route to the start line, Eddy squeezes the brakes. The mechanic comes and stands beside him. The handlebars. What height are the handlebars?

Eddy himself holds the tape measure to the stem. 'Higher.'

The mechanic loosens the bolt with a hex key and starts to raise the bars. Eddy's eyes are glued to the lines of the tape measure.

'Encore plus?' the mechanic asks.

Agonisingly slowly, the handlebars edge upwards, one millimetre at a time.

'Whoa-ho-ho. Stop!' the rider exclaims. The perfect height.

Yet there's still a hint of doubt in Eddy's eyes. What about the angle between the bars and the frame? His fingers are sheathed in white wool. It's cold enough for gloves this morning. He takes the loose handlebars between the thumb and forefinger of both hands and brings them into the right position.

The mechanic waits for a sign from the rider before he tightens them in place. Silence. For seconds that seem like minutes, Merckx's hands rest on the bars.

He scrutinises the angle once again. Now is the time: adjustments can still be made. Soon, in the heat of the race, the world will come flying past in fragments: stones, dust, a manhole cover, a dead cat, the back wheel of a heavy motorbike.

Yes. The handlebars are spot on. The mechanic is given the nod and tightens the bolt.

* * *

THE STARTING GUN is about to sound on the square in Chantilly. The peloton is ready, enveloped by a throng of cycling fans, their heroes within touching distance. Keen eyes scan the riders. There's Eddy, his shirt a shade of brown that cannot be found in any chocolatier. Connoisseurs study every detail of his bike, counting teeth in the cassette.

The click of a camera.

A tap on the shoulder.

The peloton is off. Motorbikes with cameramen perched on the back zoom around the riders. You can see it in Merckx's face: he's not happy. Are his handlebars off after all? Is there something a little out in his pedal strokes, the position of his legs, his back?

Suddenly everyone brakes. A strike. French protestors are blocking the road. A cloud with a silver lining. Merckx makes a swift about-turn and flags down a Brooklyn back-up car, the team of his rival Roger De Vlaeminck.

A hand emerges from the blue Fiat, clutching a hex key. Merckx takes a jittery look at the backs of the peloton riders. They're still stationary.

He gets off his bike and begins to tinker. He grasps the front of the saddle with his left hand and feels the texture of air-dried sausage against his palm. He slams the back of the saddle with his right and it shifts forward one millimetre. He tightens the bolt

94

beneath the faded leather. The Brooklyn mechanic gets his key back.

Merckx sets off. Cobbles rattle bikes and riders to the core. Eddy can feel the vicious edge of every stone in his backside. The saddle is a rider's sensor. Either you're sitting pretty or you're not, it's that simple.

Today Eddy is sitting anything but pretty.

*   *   *

MARC DEMEYER IS FIRST ACROSS the line in Roubaix that afternoon. Merckx scrapes sixth, looking over his shoulder as he finishes. On form, Eddy Merckx only ever looks straight ahead.

Lousy Brooklyn hex key. That one millimetre hadn't done the trick. The saddle hadn't been perfect.

Not perfect enough.

NUDE WITH WHEEL

Northern France

EVERYTHING WAS GREY. The sky, the clay, the grass. A shade that only northern France can serve up: suicide grey. A veil of murk that blots out every colour. Even my old Mercedes – a fresh olive green, or so I thought – stood sulking at the side of the road, spatters of mud along its sides.

Haveluy was the name of this stretch of cobbles, an uneven, narrow path of ancient stones, held together by grit, muck and weeds. It was November. Haveluy offered little reason to visit in autumn, or the rest of the year come to that. Except for the second Sunday in April, when the cycling classic Paris–Roubaix is run. Then the verge throngs with supporters hungry to see with their own eyes how the peloton races over the cobbles.

Half past eight in the morning. It was the photographer's idea to be here this early. Three hours ago I had picked him up in my car at his home in Vilvoorde. The photographer knew the route by heart. He and a friend had cycled the course once, a week before Paris–Roubaix.

Haveluy. The photographer could not imagine a lonelier landscape for a cyclist. That was where I'd stand in the early-morning grey. Nothingness. One man and his bike, alone in no-man's land. I could see he was right. There was nothing in Haveluy. A miracle it had ever been named at all.

FIFTEEN MINUTES AGO we had driven at a snail's pace through the local countryside. In the village of Arenberg, we even saw signs of life. A woman with her raincoat zipped up to her chin walked down the street, pulling a shopping trolley behind her. One of the wheels was refusing to cooperate. She passed a man who was waiting for the bus, his face like a potato peeled in a hurry.

The shutters of the brick houses in the former mining village of Arenberg were still closed. Every evening for years, the pitmen had hawked up phlegm into their washbasins and found coal dust; now they were jobless homebodies. The cranes that for decades had lifted the coal out of the ground still towered above the village. They had been given a fresh coat of paint: grey, of course. Tarted-up industrial heritage. Even rust would have made for a cheerier sight in these parts.

Haveluy lay four kilometres further on. A dead man's field. The perfect place to have your ashes scattered. The photographer and I took a look around. In the distance, a digger stood motionless, its claw raised to the sky. I wouldn't know where to start around here either.

I thought about vegetables. Brussels sprouts. Years ago I had set out early in the morning for a long ride across the islands of South Holland. It was chilly and I hadn't had much to eat, a combination I would live to regret. Although the route was flat, I was cycling with uphill gears. Flecks appeared in front of my eyes. This was what the peloton called 'black snow'. I got off and saw Brussels sprouts growing in a field. I pulled a few loose, rinsed them in a ditch and ate them raw. Hunger and cold, a double whammy I wouldn't wish on any cyclist.

* * *

I LIFTED MY BIKE frame out of the boot and fitted the wheels. The photographer wound a roll of film into the chamber of his Pentax. Black-and-white, naturally. This guy was old school. He wiped the lens clean on his winter jumper and peered through it at the long stretch of cobbles that dissolved into mist 100 metres further on.

'Just beautiful,' he said.

I recalled our telephone conversation of a few days ago.

'The sun is my greatest adversary,' the photographer had said.

He must have had a word with the big man in the sky about keeping things muted. The sun had clearly gone elsewhere in search of a hole in the blanket of grey. Here in Haveluy, the clouds were hanging shoulder to shoulder. I reached into the boot and pulled out a bag of cycling gear. I took off my suit. Jacket first, then trousers, followed by shirt, underpants, shoes and socks. I could feel the cold settle on my skin. It was 3°C according to the weatherman on the car radio. Hurriedly I pulled on my cycling shorts over my naked flesh, followed by a dark-blue woollen jersey, thin socks and cycling shoes.

I slithered past the Mercedes and onto the road. Through the years, the wheels of carts, cars and tractors had pressed down the cobbles on either side. The road now had a backbone that was raised a good seven inches above the rest.

'Go and stand over there, dead centre,' said the photographer.

He perched on his steel case. The first slow click emerged from his camera. He wound on the film ready for the next photo, a sight I hadn't seen in a long time.

'A little to the left. Back to the right a touch. Great.'

I stood still as a mouse. The morning chill seeped through my gear and into my chest and my thighs.

* * *

HAVELUY. I HAD BEEN HERE BEFORE, I recalled as I stared intently into the lens. I had driven over these cobbles in a back-up car as part of the Paris–Roubaix caravan a few years back, along with a fellow journalist. The organisers had graced our windscreen with a long sticker. It was a magnificent feeling: we were officially part of a cycling classic.

A small group of riders had made a break for it. The peloton was lagging a couple of minutes behind. We were between the two. The cobbles were wet. The riders would be caked in clay by the time they reached the finish. We had fairly good visibility as we drove along, flanked on either side by a human hedgerow. I saw a man with spare wheels in among the cycling fans. It was Patrick Lefevere, a Belgian team leader ready to hand out spare parts. He looked out over our passing car at the landscape behind us. Any minute now, numb with cold, the riders from his team could come speeding past.

Despite the shock absorbers, the underside of our car scraped the cobbles now and then. My Coke fizzed out of the can and over my suit. Steffen Wesemann, a German veteran and cobble specialist, fell back out of the leading group. At least, that's what the shortwave radio was saying in crackling French. We were around 200 metres behind him. A French police helicopter was hovering overhead. I had to raise my voice just to make myself heard.

'Aren't we too close?' I shouted.

'After the cobbles there's a wide stretch of tarmac. They can all pass us then,' yelled my colleague from behind the wheel.

Up ahead, a brace of motorcycles were riding over the stones. Their back wheels kept skidding out from under them. Our car had to maintain speed just to stay in balance.

In the distance I spotted a rider.

'I can see Wesemann already. When will we reach the road?'

'This is a long stretch …' said my colleague.

'See that? He's straightened up! He's going so slow we'll hit his back wheel before we know it.'

I looked over my shoulder. My stomach knotted. The peloton. A whole pack of riders was charging towards us like a herd of stampeding bulls. Spectators on either side of us were straying into the road. There was barely room to keep moving.

The peloton advanced to within 100 metres of us. The radio spat a fierce French command. 'Car 213. Get out of there. Out!'

On our windscreen I read the three numbers on the sticker, back to front.

'They mean us. We've got to get out of here.'

There was little doubt that the helicopter crew above had us in their sights.

Left and right, cycling fans jumped back onto the verge at the last moment so as not to be hit by the car. Up ahead, Wesemann was falling further back. From behind, the peloton was bearing down. There was no way out.

'Car 213. Get out. Now!'

My colleague was doing double take after double take between the rear-view mirror and the road ahead. Behind us, race directors were blasting their car horns. The helicopter swooped 100 metres above the course.

We saw Wesemann fish something to eat out of the back pocket of his filthy shirt. We were too far away to see what he had in his hand. Behind us a discordant chorus of klaxons rang out.

'Car 213. *Exclu!*'

Exclu. We were banished from the race. A motorcyclist appeared at my window. Wild gesticulation. Incoherent barks from beneath his black helmet. We had to follow him. What else could we do? He rode his motorcycle brazenly into the crowd, which parted to create a gap for our car. My colleague steered us as far into the empty space on the verge as he could.

A pair of police motorbikes and a snazzy official race car tore past on our left, followed immediately by the peloton. An angry rider thumped the roof of our car.

The motorcyclist was still standing motionless in front of us. Without stirring from his saddle he removed the glove from his hand. With his nails he picked at the sticker on our windscreen. One tug and it was loose.

'*Exclu!*' he shouted, redundantly. In no uncertain terms he made it clear that we were to leave the course at the end of this stretch.

Once all the team leaders' cars had passed, the motorcyclist led us over the cobbles. A gendarme at the side of the road signalled to us to turn off. As every pair of eyes along the roadside strained to follow the last of the riders, we exited the course.

Nothing else for it but to take the long way round on the main road to the finish at Roubaix.

* * *

'WE COULD TRY IT NUDE,' said the photographer. 'With a spare wheel in your hand.'

'Yeah? Is that what you want?' I answered, pondering his request.

'I caught a look at you when you were getting changed behind the car. I can see it in my mind's eye. From the back, okay?'

Back. My back. My backside. My arse. Two white arse cheeks on the cobbles of Haveluy.

'Okay,' I said.

We readied ourselves. The photographer painstakingly picked out exactly the right location. I leaned against my old Mercedes, waiting for the sign to disrobe.

A cyclist is a sportsman of two halves. The bottom half is overdeveloped. The legs get virtually no rest during all those miles on the road, while the glutes and lower back have to generate power and stability throughout the race. The shoulders and the rest of the upper body are more of an appendage. A swimmer's torso is enormous. Seen from behind, he's a capital V on legs. The cyclists who can flash a bit of muscle in a short-sleeved shirt are few and far between. Bulging biceps might help you tug a little harder on the handlebars but that's not going to win you any races. It's all about that powerhouse of thighs and buttocks.

'I'm ready,' said the photographer. 'If you get too cold, slip into my coat while I'm changing rolls.'

'Never mind. Too much hassle. I'll survive.'

If only he knew how much I hate the cold.

I shed my cycling togs, shoes and socks last, and scurried naked over the cobbles to the spot indicated by the photographer, some ten metres from the lens. The mud squidged up between my toes. Black peanut butter.

The photographer began to give directions. Wheel in your left hand. No, wait, your right hand. How about both hands. Above your head. Try swinging it in one hand. Sit on it. Hold it in front of you. Er … no, behind you.

This went on for 15 minutes. I tried to visualise what the photographer was looking at. He must have noticed the sinewy calves, inherited from my father. Every morning, in the cold store of his company on the Coolhaven in Rotterdam, Dad used to stack boxes in temperatures of −20°C. Boxes of meat, hotdogs, ice cream, chips. Funny how, as the son of a deep-freeze wholesaler, I had developed such an intense loathing of the cold.

With my bare feet I sized up the aged stones. Unwieldy, immovable old bastards, settled in their spot and not about to give an inch – ever. I could feel their uneven surface through the hard skin on my soles.

What a nightmare to have to chase over this stretch of cobbles at a speed of over 50kmph. 'Floating above the spine of the path in a heavy gear' – that's how the best always claimed it should be done. Bernard Hinault, the pride of Brittany, initially refused to give Paris–Roubaix a go. He dismissed it as an insane and hellish ordeal. Hinault was scared to fall, scared to lose. Falling and losing: a cyclist's two greatest fears. Apart from being caught for doping. In 1981, his hunger for glory got the better of him and he eventually won the race he had despised for so long.

* * *

BY NOW THE NUDE PHOTOSHOOT had gone way past the 15-minute mark. The cold was slicing straight through my skin and into my bones, or so it seemed. My buttocks began to tremble, as if the photographer was administering jolts of electricity to make them jiggle up and down. Shifting my weight from one foot to the other, I was able to make the trembling subside for a second or two.

My manhood was already seeking shelter from the icy wind. You can read a lot into the length of a cock. I've heard it called a thermostat for sensation and temperature. Looking down, I observed that conditions were far from favourable.

'Hold it there. Shift your weight onto your left hip. Get the wheel a little closer to your leg.'

In Florence, Michelangelo's *David* has been leaning on his right leg for over 500 years. His left knee is bent and his right hand dangles a little awkwardly next to his thigh, his massive fingers curled. How long did the model have to hold that pose before the sculptor was all chiselled out?

My left buttock was now trembling relentlessly, as if it was having a chuckle at my expense. Enjoying a private joke with the photographer behind my back.

'Can you hang your head a little more? Make it a little sadder? Yes, that's it.'

A naked man in a suicide-grey no-man's land.

HYPOTHERMIA ROBS PEOPLE OF THEIR ABILITY TO THINK. I'd read it somewhere. They start hallucinating. I hadn't quite reached that stage yet. These cobbled roads were not made with endless contemplation in mind.

In the distance, the digger began to move. Its claw lowered steadily. Behind me I could hear the sporadic click of the camera. The photographer must have immortalised my arse countless times by now; I'd been standing here for half an hour. Only a few seconds had been captured on film. The rest had vanished into thin air.

Judging by the noise, the digger was heading our way. There was no explaining to a French farmer what we were doing here. An old Mercedes, doors and boot open wide, a naked man with a wheel in his hand being urged on by another man brandishing a camera. I'd have called the local coppers long ago.

'I can't keep this up much longer,' I said, cupping my right hand over my scrotum to shield it from the cold. My balls were retreating into my underbelly in search of warmer climes.

'Just hold it there a second. This is beautiful.'

It was a second too much. I'd sacrificed enough for beauty.

'Have you got a good one?' I asked the photographer.

He thought he had.

'Then we're stopping,' I said.

I walked towards him as if going in search of my clothes on a muddy stretch of cobbles at half past nine on a November morning was the most normal thing in the world. Quick as I could, I pulled on anything within reach. I didn't care what as long as it could give me warmth.

* * *

THE ENGINE OF THE STATIONARY CAR was running to get the heater up to speed. I was looking a treat in my mix-and-match outfit, from the cycling gloves on my frozen fingers to the polished toecaps of my pointy boots.

The bike and the photographer's case were tucked away in the boot.

'Job well done?' I asked.

'Yes. Perfect,' said the photographer.

I shifted the gearstick into the D for 'drive' and we lumbered over the cobbles back to civilisation.

* * *

AFTER OUR BANISHMENT from the race – we must have yelled *exclu!* a thousand times on the way to Roubaix – my partner in crime and I pulled into the car park at the Roubaix vélodrome. Our press passes gave us access. The stands around the concrete cycle track were packed with fans, eagerly awaiting the arrival of the first rider. The blue lane at the bottom, dubbed the Côte d'Azur, had been given a fresh lick of paint. Once a year the track dolled itself up, like an elderly spinster about to be reunited with an old flame and rummaging in her handbag for her blue eyeshadow.

When the race was over, we walked alongside the riders as they cycled at a funereal pace towards the washroom. They handed their bikes over to their *mécaniciens* and went inside. It was a run-down space, 10 by 15 metres, with a shower for every rider, divided by terrazzo partitions. Without the least embarrassment they stripped off their filthy gear and stepped under the shower.

I could see grazes on hips, knees and arms. Hands covered in liquid soap rubbed them over once or twice; that must really sting. Whirlpools of water, mud, blood and spit formed around the drains. After a race like this there's not a single rider who thinks twice about letting his piss flow freely. This room, with its grey stone partitions, almost seemed built for the purpose. In this setting, a row of pigs awaiting slaughter would not have looked out of place.

A steady stream of stragglers continued to arrive, smeared with the grey mud of the region. Losers with a story hardly anyone wanted to hear. In the warmth of the sports arena down the hall, the freshly showered winner was already snug in his tracksuit chatting to the press.

* * *

THE PHOTOGRAPHER AND I HAD LEFT THE COBBLES of Haveluy behind us and were driving back to Belgium. The heating dial on the dashboard was set to the fattest red star and finally I was beginning to warm up. We crossed the border, leaving northern France for what it was.

'Could you turn down the radio so I can call home?' the photographer asked.

I barely listened in on his conversation. I was thinking back to the cobbles of Haveluy. Odd that you can't remember the cold, only the fact that it was cold. My time in the cold had been reduced to a roll or two of black-and-white film.

The photographer hung up. 'There's spuds in garlic butter waiting for us at home.'

'Great,' I said. 'I'm starving.'

106

Grey clouds filled the rear-view mirror. The dashboard clock said 11 o'clock. The sky had lightened up, but not by much. A cemetery flashed past at the side of the motorway.

'Look at all those flowers on the graves,' I said.

They were garish in the grey of the day. I suspected they were plastic.

'Today is the day of the dead,' said the photographer.

'Huh?'

'The day of the dead. All Souls' Day. People visit the grave of a loved one, clean it up and lay fresh flowers.' I couldn't remember ever having laid a bunch of flowers on a grave.

* * *

THE PHOTOGRAPHER AND I ARRIVED at the place where the spuds lay waiting in the fridge. Stiff as two boards, we clambered out of the car. It was warm in the kitchen. The photographer put the potatoes in the oven and before long the aroma of garlic was everywhere. I caught sight of myself in the full-length mirror. Looking back was a rag-tag figure in boots and leggings, jumper piled upon jumper.

The glass oven dish appeared on the table. The spuds, split lengthways and oozing butter, sizzled side by side.

Before long I would be plunged into developer in an old-fashioned darkroom on the day of the dead. Gradually, second by second, my naked self would emerge from the magic paper. A living man clutching a wheel, stones beneath his bare feet. Quick. In the stop bath. Fix the image. A rider seeking the end of a cobbled road.

A rider with no clothes, no spectators, nothing to eat or drink. Not a breath of heat, no title to his name.

A rider worth nothing at all.

Solo

Netherlands

I PREFER TO CYCLE ALONE. Solo. Seize the moment, grab my bike and strike out from home. Cycling as a solitary pursuit. A landscape, a bike, a full water bottle, a muesli bar in my back pocket and I'm all set.

But catching sight of another rider in the distance, something takes hold of me. I have to see how I measure up.

So here I am. It's a sunny afternoon and a red-shirted cyclist is a good 200 metres ahead of me. I start to pick up my pace and watch the distance shrink. I'm already close enough to gauge the rotation of his pedals.

His tempo is slower than mine, that's for sure.

My front wheel is only a few metres from his back wheel. I take a good look at his gears. His chain is driving the small chainring, no match for my bigger gear.

Time to up the speed and glide past him with the friendly nod riders exchange in passing. Now I can look forward to pushing on alone. A few powerful strokes of the pedals later, I glance over my shoulder. He's dawdling behind.

I am alone again.

Two hours into my route from Rotterdam via Vlist and Schoon-hoven, I arrive at a junction. The traffic light for cyclists is red. It's a busy crossing and it takes a while for the cars to trickle away.

With the tip of my shoe on the bike path, I stretch my aching back. I've been barrelling along at too high a tempo again. Will I ever learn not to overestimate my own strength?

My front wheel is on the white line and while I've been waiting a group of cyclists has gathered around me. From behind I hear the drone of a stationary engine.

The little green cyclist lights up.

From standing, I want to be the first to get up to speed. The faster I take off, the sooner I'll be back in my state of choice: solo.

My flying start goes according to plan; most cyclists are happy to ease into their first metres. Not me: my shoes are already clipped into the pedals and acceleration is my middle name. A swift and steady rise through 20, 25, 30kmph.

Behind me I hear an engine revving, the same one as back at the lights. I take a quick look over my shoulder: a moped with two people in the saddle. Now, there are few things finer when your legs are weary than sliding into the slipstream of another rider. A joy that's up there with my love of cycling alone.

In anticipation, I shift up a gear. Only seconds now till I'm being carried along. The moped growls past me. A man at the helm, boy on the back – father and son is my guess – suspension sagging deep under their combined weight. Once they're in front of me I slot in behind, my wheel almost up against their mudguard to gain the full effect of the suction.

The tail-light is shining brightly despite the glare of the afternoon sun.

A curly blond ponytail is sticking out from under the boy's helmet. I can make out part of the driver's face as he keeps an eye on me in both rear-view mirrors. Beefy, double chin. He turns his head to the side and shouts to the boy behind him. I can't catch the gist of it.

The boy turns his head and studies the distance between us. I flash him a friendly smile, being sure to keep my front wheel within striking distance of the mudguard.

Two become one, a harmonious unit speeding its way over the B road that will take us to the Algera Bridge across the River IJssel. Drafting, it's called in cycling jargon, the sublime suction you feel behind the broad back of another cyclist. Drafting behind a moped takes it to a higher, faster level.

The boy continues to stare at my front wheel. He says something to the man in front of him and turns around again.

'What are you playing at?' he yells.

My jaw drops. There was me thinking they saw the fun in me tagging along in their slipstream.

'What d'you mean?' I shout back.

'Piss off!'

'What's up?'

'Don't cycle so fast.'

'Fast? I'm barely doing 30.'

The boy's face turns red with anger.

'If you don't piss off now ...'

'Take it easy,' I say. 'I'm not breaking any laws.'

The boy turns back to the driver. He eyes me up in his mirrors, beefy face fit to burst.

I shift up another gear and cycle past them.

'Better now?' I ask.

I can imagine their frustration at a racing bike outpacing their precious moped. I don't have to imagine long. When I smile back at them, the boy rises from the saddle and looks daggers at me. Just as I'm deciding that full speed ahead is the best policy, I hear them ease up on the throttle. They're taking a right.

'Arsehole!' the boy shouts as they veer off down an underpass.

'What the hell's wrong with you?' I yell back.

I see the driver hesitate, wondering whether to turn around and come after me. I feel a shot of adrenalin and bear down on the pedals.

Shit! Let's hope they're not the kind of nutters to pull a gun … Just to be sure I dip a little lower and ride like the blazes. When I reach the turn-off for the bridge, I dare to look back at last: they're nowhere to be seen.

The adrenalin is coursing through my veins.

Relax. Deep breaths. No big deal. Just a couple of whack jobs, ignore them.

I climb to the highest point of the bridge. Settling into my descent, I finally start to feel at ease again. My right eye starts to fill up in the strong wind and I wipe a tear from my cheek. Not far from home now. I take a swallow from my bottle, hit a nice tight rhythm and the reddish-brown of the bike path flashes along beneath me.

No one ahead, no one behind.

The blessing of riding solo.

BLACK FEATHERS

Netherlands

Coots. I RECOGNISED THEIR AWKWARD PITTER-PATTER from a long way off. Two coots, a pair most likely, making their jaunty way across the bike path. A strip of asphalt three metres wide. No cars allowed. Mr and Mrs Coot had all the time in the world.

The wind was at my back. Even without pedalling my speed held steady. An invisible hand was pushing me back into town on the final loop of my weekly cycle.

It was breeding season. Along the way I had seen all kinds of birds toiling away with twigs and bits of straw. Grebes, ducks, moorhens. Coots like to build floating nests. They think they're safe out there on the water.

What made these two coots decide to go walkabout at this very spot? Was there food to be had?

The bike path was lined with villas. In recent years a host of detached residences had sprung up. Those with money to spare were escaping the chaos of Rotterdam and opting for a home with a view, overlooking the tranquil waters of the river that gives the city its name.

Fifty metres to go. Time for my feathered friends to get a bit of a move on.

'Shoo! Shoo!' I yelled.

The coot in front made a movement that could only signal shock. The coot bringing up the rear did a U-turn, pattered off and dived from the narrow verge back into the water. Thirty metres and counting.

There he stood on the asphalt: a creature wracked by doubt. A vacillating coot. I could tell by his body language that he was weighing up his options: advance or retreat?

Twenty metres left. The bird raised his right leg and put it down in exactly the same spot. He did nothing and kept staring in my direction.

'Vamoose!' I shouted. It was far too human a cry. The coot froze solid. I slammed on the brakes.

I'd seen a TV show about how far a car travels once the driver has hit the brakes. It turns out motorists are way too optimistic about how long it takes to screech to a halt, ascribing supernatural powers to their brakes and seriously underestimating their speed. Only when you see a collision played back in slow motion can you fully appreciate the forces of destruction it unleashes.

My braking distance was too long. Brake pads squealed against rims and my back wheel skidded out from under me. Startled by the noise, the coot huddled down, his legs disappearing under his plumage.

I tried to steer clear of him. Left or right?

Where is a coot's crumple zone?

The bird tucked his head down and seemed to be waiting for the inevitable, his beady eyes staring right at me. One metre to go. The coot took an unexpected leap, a last-ditch dive for escape. In the wrong direction.

There was no stopping now.

My front wheel ran over his rib cage at high speed. I lost my balance and struggled to stay upright. Black feathers flew through the air. Wings rattled against my spokes. I had to swivel not to fall. The coot turned along with my front wheel, wedged between spokes and fork. I lost control of the bike. With the bird caught in the fork, my front wheel jammed and my back wheel left the ground. I let go of the brakes and the coot flopped onto the asphalt beneath my pedals.

Black on black.

Before I could make another move, my back wheel had run him over. I heard a crack, as if I had pulled on a roast chicken leg and twisted hard: the sound of bone shooting free of flesh.

I ground to a halt a few metres further on, in the middle of the bike path. I looked behind me. The bird lay motionless.

Dead?

A few last downy feathers came to rest beside the coot. His head lay at a peculiar angle. My heart was pounding in the back of my throat. I turned my bike around and cycled back. An eye, half open but apparently lifeless, seemed to look right through me. It reminded me of the boy next-door's lazy eye when his mum took off his patch before bedtime: dazed, no focus.

Slowly the coot's left wing rose from the asphalt. A final spasm? The quills splayed in all directions, at the mercy of the wind. The wing sank back onto the ground.

I looked around. What are you supposed to do after a collision with a water bird? Call animal rescue? The coot and I found ourselves next to a villa with a freshly thatched roof. No sign of anyone at the windows.

From the river I could hear a short sharp wail emanating from a bird's throat, repeating every few seconds. Mrs Coot appeared from behind a bed of reeds, paddling restlessly to and fro in the water.

When is a bird dead? I had seen people die. Changes in skin colour and the onset of rigor mortis let you know that life is leaving the body, like a genie escaping from a bottle. At a loved one's deathbed, the difference between still alive and newly deceased is unmistakable. In an animal, I didn't know what to look for.

Was the coot's brain still sending signals to its mangled body or was I looking at a crumbled edifice of bones and feathers? His crushed ribcage was no longer moving. I had to convince myself that the bird was dead. Half-heartedness would be nothing short of culpable.

I nudged the bird's head with the toe of my cycling shoe. His beak opened a little.

Alive. Shit!

I took a firm hold of my handlebars and rolled the front wheel over the coot's neck, back and forth, back and forth. To my horror, a wing began to flap again. The last little bit of life? To make sure, I flattened his neck once more beneath my wheel. The wing flapped again. Less noticeably this time but still clearly visible.

It occurred to me that perhaps all I was doing was obstructing the coot's breathing. To put him out of his misery I would have to crush his skull. I lifted my front wheel off the ground and slammed it down on his head a few times. Fragments of his white frontal shield now lay on the asphalt. Blood was flowing from his open beak. His eye was pulverised. A coot without a face. Total loss, the insurance man would say if this were a car. The bird was a write-off.

Adrenalin surged through my body. This must be how a murderer feels delivering the fatal blow to a mutilated victim.

This was death, yes. The coot was dead. I was sure. Very sure. I stifled the urge to throw up.

I had blundered into the role of a criminal. What should I do with the body? Drape a white handkerchief over it? Drag it by its legs into the undergrowth? I caught a whiff of myself. This was not the sweat of cycling. This was the sweat of fear.

I took another look around. No one in sight. The only sound was the piercing cry of Mrs Coot, keeping her beady eye on me from the water.

I couldn't just leave the mangled creature lying there on the ground. No one would be any the wiser if I tossed his body into the reeds by the riverbank. I looked at the female coot, paddling anxiously around. There was no point in projecting human emotions onto an animal. I knew that. But I still didn't have the heart to chuck a dead coot at a live one.

The front garden of the thatched villa bordered on the bike path and suddenly I noticed that it had recently been dug over. The soil had yet to be flattened and was still loose. I laid my bike at the edge of the path and lifted the limp coot up by the legs. His bloodied head dangled to and fro above the asphalt.

Carefully I laid the bird on the loose soil and began to dig furiously. It was light work. A few determined scrapes of the hand and I'd reached the right depth. I picked the coot up and placed him in the hollow. He lay there contentedly, his legs drooping over his plumage and his little head bowed forward, peaceful as an old man in a black cardie who's nodded off in front of the telly.

As I filled in the hole with the soil I'd clawed aside, I looked up and saw two cyclists off in the distance, heading my way. Hastily I patted down the earth; you could hardly tell it had been disturbed. I raked my fingers over the surface just to be sure.

The two cyclists were approaching at considerable speed. Their shirts bore the names of major cycling sponsors, Sky and Leopard.

I dusted off my fingers on my shorts and positioned my bike ready for the off. For appearances' sake I fiddled with a brake pad on my back wheel. From among the reeds, alarming cries were still emanating from the throat of the female coot. I reckoned it was high time she packed it in.

Behind me I heard the ping of a bicycle bell. The same high-pitched sound you hear when a chef has finished plating up and slides a meal under the infrared lamp to keep warm.

The two men whizzed past me. The one in the rear, wearing the Sky shirt, peered over his shoulder. Was he wondering what was up with my bike? We held each other's gaze for a second before he hunched over again and pedalled determinedly after his cycling buddy.

Had he seen me digging?

I looked at the spot where the bird was interred. As a boy I would have made a better job of the burial and cobbled together a cross from sticks and a rubber band. Now an unmarked grave was the expedient choice. Nothing more to be done: it was an accident, pure and simple. Bad luck. Kismet.

The female coot floated silently on the water. She had stopped wailing but she was still giving me the evil eye.

The path was deserted. The two cyclists had disappeared from view. As I pushed off with my free foot, my eyes were drawn to the living room window of the villa. Through a chink in the net curtains I made out the contours of a face and a mop of grey hair. Was that a woman peering out? How long had she been standing there? I turned away sharpish and sped off as fast as my legs would go. I didn't dare look back.

FAST-FORWARD: one week later, around the same time, noon-ish. The weather had taken a turn for the better. You could already smell summer in the air.

I looked down at my front wheel as I cycled my familiar route along the path by the River Rotte. I had used a scouring sponge and hot water to wash away the splashes of red on the rubber profile of my tyre. A wipe or two and all the blood was gone. One final piece of evidence to be disposed of: I threw the sponge into the bin and changed the bag straight away. It was only the next day when the dustbin men whacked the bag into the gaping maw of the garbage truck that I knew all traces had been obliterated.

The lovely weather had brought the water birds out in force. I saw a grebe slide beneath the surface in one fluid motion. I was cycling too fast to see where it reappeared. I spotted a nest among the reeds next to a drawbridge. A coot was brooding, her head raised and alert. Were there eggs tucked away beneath her feathers?

The thatched roof of the villa appeared in the distance. To avoid being recognised I had exchanged my blue Italian kit for an older Acqua e Sapone jersey, bright red. I was also sporting sunglasses, not strictly necessary under a blanket of light cloud.

I rounded a bend and saw the villa in its entirety.

A headwind. I shifted to a lighter gear and had to pick up the pace to maintain my speed. Less than 200 metres to go. How often had I breezed through this section of my Sunday cycle without a care in the world? Now I was clocking every detail: the verge, the bushes, the span of the river, the lampposts, the bed of reeds.

A jeep and trailer were parked beside the villa. Thirty metres to go. I eased up on the pedals and slowed down. Bold capitals on the back of the trailer proclaimed VAN WEELDEN, LANDSCAPE ARCHITECTS. A man in overalls was leaning against the side of the jeep, mobile phone pressed to his ear. As he spoke, he kicked his heels against the rear tyre and clods of earth fell to the ground.

I tilted my head to the side. Towards the grave. The coot's final resting place. My eyes scanned the garden. No expanse of loose, dark soil, yet I knew this must be the place. Then the realisation dawned: bright-green turf had been laid over the top. I could see the seams running between the sods.

Along the side of the house, they had left space for a border. A young lad in overalls was down on his knees, digging little holes in the soil. Next to him was a wooden crate packed with vivid orange marigolds.

A set of garden furniture graced the middle of the brand-new lawn. A woman was sitting on one of the chairs, reading. I took one look at the mop of grey hair peeping out above the cover of her magazine and began to pedal like mad.

Where the lawn met the bike path, something caught my eye: two glass bowls in the grass. I took a peek as I sped on past. They contained neatly sliced pieces of white bread, crusts removed.

The villa lay behind me. Despite the persistent headwind I switched up a gear. On my left, the reeds swayed to and fro. Coots were paddling up and down the river. More than I had ever seen before.

FARMER ON THE ROAD

Netherlands

THE NARROW PATH STRETCHED for miles through a landscape I had only ever seen in paintings by the Dutch Masters. The leaves were an intense green that had fled the city years ago. Cycling across a narrow bridge, I looked down to see the plants on the riverbed waving up at me. That's how clear the water was.

What misguided Dutchman had called this region the Achterhoek, a name that dismissed it as some deprived corner of the back of beyond? Today it struck me as the heart of something precious.

The day was nowhere near its height but already I was wishing I'd slapped on some sun cream. A bird of prey traced a slow circle high above, wings motionless, a glider on the updraughts. I stopped to take a better look, shielding my eyes from the glare. The bird continued its unruffled gyre, on the lookout for prey.

I was thirsty. My bottle was filled with tap water from the holiday home I had rented in the little town of Ruurlo. I swallowed down a couple of mouthfuls. The taste was almost sweet. Just as I was returning the bottle to its holder, I heard a pair of clogs dragging across the ground. I looked to one side and saw a farmer walking across his yard to the road. Behind him stood a row of cows in an open barn, heads bowed over the hay.

The farmer clacked up to me.

'So-o-o, out training?' he said with an Achterhoek drawl.

'Yup,' I replied.

One of the cows mooed and tried to wrestle her head free of the collar around her neck. To no avail. The other cows didn't so much as blink, grinding hay between their jaws and dipping their noses in the water trough.

'Do you only keep cows?'

'Got two goats behind the barn. And a horse out in the field. But yeah, mainly just cows. Getting on for 40.'

'Is that a lot?' I asked.

'Nah, nothing to write home about. Last year milk was selling at 25 cents a litre. Not what you'd call a living wage.'

My hands were itching to tame the farmer's wiry grey hair. It was sticking up in all directions, a tangle of frayed rope crying out for a good seeing-to with a steel brush.

A dog came wandering over, swatting shiny green flies with its tail. The pudgy mutt took a sniff at my cycling shoes, rubbed up against my calf once or twice and lay down next to me on the warm asphalt. Its coat reminded me of the farmer's hair and my urge to grab a brush grew stronger. Perhaps it was just a deep-seated desire to have a great big bush of hair on my own billiard ball of a head – the joy of tugging hard bristles through it and feeling the stripes they left on my scalp.

'Tough times for Dutch farmers,' I answered, not really knowing what I meant by it.

The dog's tail swept to and fro across its back. A bunch of flies took off, only to land on exactly the same spot.

'And to cap it all there was the divorce last year,' said the farmer, playing his trump card. He gazed past me along the road.

A divorce. Behind the cowshed stood a typical Achterhoek farmhouse with two massive stable doors at the back.

The farmer still wasn't looking at me. He took a deep breath. 'Shitty year all told.'

The dog had heard it all before and kept its eyes firmly shut.

'Where's your wife now?'

'Gone.'

'Someone else?'

'Got that right.'

'From around here?'

'Nah, Naaldwijk. She lives in Naaldwijk now. Six years she'd been seeing him.'

He coughed without opening his mouth.

'Got him off the internet,' he said.

The farmer's hands hung at his sides. Slime from the mouths of his cows had streaked his overalls and glued a few yellow stalks to the sleeves.

'Jeeez ...'

'Yeah, didn't see that one coming. Did we, Shep?'

The dog half-raised one eyelid. And slowly let it droop again.

'And my own daughter never breathed a word ...'

'She was living at home?'

The farmer nodded. 'Must've known about the whole mucky business. Known for years. She's 20 now. Studying to be a lab assistant in Leiden.'

My bike was standing immobile between my legs. I ran a finger across my brow to wipe away the sweat. The sun was beating down.

'Dog won't touch you,' said the farmer. 'Will you, Shep?'

There we stood. A man and his dog. A man and his bike. You could tell the days to come would only be hotter. Long cracks ran through the dry soil in the fields around us.

There was no traffic on the narrow path. Hardly a breath of wind. The only sound was the hiss of cars speeding along the dual carriageway in the distance.

'Racing bike?' asked the farmer, pointing his nose at my Masciaghi.

'Yeah, I'm in training. Off to Italy on holiday in a few weeks. Taking the bike with me.'

The farmer wasn't listening. He laughed soundlessly, little more than a tightening of the mouth. 'But I've got a girlfriend now myself. No flies on me. Got her off the internet too.'

I reckoned he must be well into his sixties, with a stoop no chiropractor could mend and grey hairs sprouting from his damp nostrils. Did this man really have a girlfriend? Surely she would have taken the scissors to those nose hairs by now?

I looked up at the bird of prey, still circling high above the farm. It had a mighty wingspan.

'Buzzard,' said the farmer. 'Usually sits over there in the bare treetops. Flies his rounds every now and then. Must be wondering what those two blokes are doing on the road with a dog lying next to them.'

A couple of cowshed residents clanged their chains against the iron railing. 'I still milk them every day. By hand.'

'My cousin over in Hazerswoude milks his cows by computer,' I said. 'He's got a screen at home that tells him how much milk they produce a day and how much feed they need.'

The farmer's eyes met mine at last. 'I want nothing to do with those new-fangled milking machines. I do it all by hand.'

'And right you are,' I said in the hope of bringing our little chat to a close.

When I clipped my left shoe into the pedal, the dog woke with a start, heaved its body up onto its stiff legs and shook its woolly belly.

'Don't train too hard,' said the farmer. He tapped the heel of his right clog on the asphalt and a dry clump of earth fell from it. The dog took a good sniff.

I pushed off with my right foot. When I was settled on the saddle, I looked over my shoulder.

The farmer was still standing in the road. He stuck his palm in the air and held it there, a good old-fashioned manly wave. The dog slouched back into the yard. I waved back and picked up my pace.

When I arrived at the bare trees I took a look up. The buzzard was slumped on a thick branch. No plans for the rest of the day, by the look of him.

Flat

Netherlands

Frenzied barking erupted on the other side of the door. Then came the scrabbling of sharp nails on wood. I took my finger off the bell and backed away.

A woman's voice.

'Spanky!'

The barking grew louder.

'Down, Spanky! Down!'

The door of the wooden chalet swung open to reveal a woman on a coconut doormat straining to hold back a wild-eyed mutt. Her tangle of blonde hair had been pulled back into a ponytail and a tight pink jogging suit was struggling to contain her ample curves. She straightened up and the word LOVE spangled across her breasts.

'What d'you want?' she asked, fixing me with enquiring blue eyes and tightening her grip on the dog's collar. It was a bull terrier. I'd recognise those piggish features anywhere.

Once, at a high school party, I had been bitten by an exact replica of the dog I was facing. It had bounded over and leapt up at me just as I was about to tuck into a meat-paste sandwich. When I tried to fend it off, it sank its teeth into my hand. Ever since, I'd walk a mile to avoid a bull terrier. Pretty much any dog, come to that.

'Uh, I'm doing a spot of cycling,' I said.

'You don't say,' the woman answered, eyeing up my wet cycling shorts and bare shins without a hint of embarrassment. My bike was leaning against the garden fence behind me, rain bouncing off the saddle.

'I've got a flat tyre. I have a repair kit with me but I was wondering if you have a bicycle pump I could borrow?'

The woman puffed out her cheeks and exhaled slowly. 'Let me take a look.'

The floor in the hallway was covered in yellow linoleum that curled up at the skirting boards. Through an open door, I caught sight of a bed and two sleeping bags.

The woman dragged the dog into the bedroom by its collar and slammed the door. The barking reached a new crescendo.

'He was vicious when we got him,' she shrugged. 'Anyone else would've had him put down by now.'

I nodded.

She opened a cupboard next to the coat stand and reached in past a couple of bin bags that were overflowing with clothes. Her exertions exposed a strip of white flesh above her waistline.

'Well, whaddaya know,' she exclaimed triumphantly, re-emerging with a bicycle pump held aloft. It was mounted on a little wooden plank.

'Great!' I smiled. 'Just what I was looking for.'

I set the pump down on the floor and had a go at the plunger. A few little balls of fluff rolled along the skirting board.

'Bring your bike inside. It's really pissing it down out there.'

'That's very kind of you. I'll be 15 minutes, tops.'

'Don't rush on my account,' she answered. 'I'm not going anywhere.'

* * *

RESTING ON THE SADDLE AND HANDLEBARS, my upturned bike was a tight fit in the hallway. I started feeling my way along the profile of the tyre in search of a splinter of glass or a sharp stone. Find that and I'd found my puncture. The gears clicked as I spun the wheel and the tyre slid through my palm. Nothing. Nice and smooth.

The woman had gone into the living room and was standing with her back to me. She had sturdy hips and a tasty roll of fat was peeping over the waist of her pink jogging pants. A cloud of cigarette smoke floated above her blonde hair.

I fished my repair kit from my cycling shirt, took out two tyre levers and stuck them one after the other between the tyre and the rim. Carefully I eased out the inner tube.

Can of Coke in one hand and fag in the other, the woman came over and stood next to me. She puffed out a stream of smoke.

'How's it going?' she asked.

I had screwed an adapter onto the valve and pumped a little air into the inner tube.

'Fine. Just trying to locate the puncture.'

The sound of my voice set the dog off again.

'Jeeezus, Spanky. Shut the fuck up, will yer!'

The dog's outburst meant I couldn't hear the air escape. I held the tube close to my ear and felt it slowly soften.

'Nice little place you've got here. Still on holiday?' I asked.

The woman dropped her smouldering fag end into the Coke can.

'Nah, me and my fella live here all year round. Against the rules, like. It's supposed to be just for the summer but … As long as nobody complains, right?'

A mobile phone in her jogging pants went off. I saw the display light up through the material. She put the can down on a shelf beneath the hall mirror and answered.

'Babs! Hiya. Where are you?'

(…)

'Traffic jam? Where?'

(…)

'But it's due to start any minute.'

She wandered back into the living room. 'Yeah, get a move on,' she continued. 'I'll never get that thing running on my own.'

The dog had shut up at last. I pumped up the inner tube and held it to my ear again.

'Don't get a fright if there's a fella in the hall when you get here. He needed a pump.'

(…)

'Yeah, yeah. Very funny, Babs.'

She paced the length of the room and back, cackling loudly.

'Nah, Jim's away. On call. Should be back around nine. Broken lift in an office down Dordt way.'

(…)

'All right then, see you in a bit.'

She slid the phone back in her pocket, pulled the rubber band from her ponytail, shook her hair loose and swept it back into place again. Then she disappeared from view. I heard the sound of rummaging followed by an almighty smack. She had walloped something.

'Useless pile of crap,' she snarled.

The doorbell sounded above my head and the dog went mad again. The woman in the living room seemed to be in no hurry, so I did the honours. What the …? For a second I thought my hostess had climbed out the living-room window and rung the bell for a laugh. The woman before me was identical except that the pink jogging suit had been traded for a red one. Even the word LOVE jiggled on her breasts.

The lady in red took a step towards me, hand outstretched: 'Hiya, I'm Barbara.'

Twins. Like her sister, Barbara wore her blonde hair in a pony-tail. She had the same ample figure, the same complexion, teeth, eyes. Only her lips were noticeably fuller.

'Flat tyre, eh? Erna was just saying,' she said.

I nodded. 'Yes. Won't be in your way long.'

Barbara squeezed past the bike and strolled into the living room. I heard the smacking of lips as they kissed hello. Cautiously I peeked my head round the door.

'Sorry, but could I trouble you for a basin of water? I'm having trouble finding the hole.'

Barbara cocked an eyebrow and headed for the kitchen. I heard the banging of cupboard doors and she returned with a washing-up basin.

'You can fill it in the loo.'

As I half-filled the basin with water, I heard their raised voices in the living room, punctuated by more loud bangs. It sounded like they were taking turns to lay into something.

'Aw, Christ! They'll have started by now.'

'Bleedin' useless!'

I could barely tell them apart.

Kneeling beside the basin, I immersed the inner tube in water. After inspecting a quarter of its length, I finally spotted a tiny string of bubbles rising to the surface. I'd found my puncture! I turned the valve, let the air escape and sank my teeth into the rubber to mark the spot.

'Could you mebbe give us a hand?'

The sisters were parked side by side in the doorway. Pink and red: a garish but cheerful combo.

'What can I do for you?'

'We need to use the computer but we can't get it to work,' Erna, the pink sister, answered.

I followed them into the living room. The air was damp, the windows had fogged up.

A boxy grey monitor and a yellowed keyboard were sitting on a camping table, hooked up to a computer on the floor. A clutch of cables emerged from the back and ran along the skirting.

'Haven't seen one of these in a while,' I said.

'Yeah, we don't have much use for it. Prefer the telly, really.'

The computer seemed to be running. I could hear the sound of the cooling fan.

'It's humming. That's a good sign,' I bluffed. I wasn't about to let on that changing a light bulb unaided was a decent result in my book.

The screen was dark. I got down on my knees and checked the cable that connected the computer to the monitor. Nothing wrong that I could see. I turned my attention to the multiple socket on the floor. One of the plugs looked as if it had taken a knock. Its wires were exposed. I stood up and yanked the cable. The screen flickered.

'Might be something up with the plug.'

The twins looked at me sheepishly. Clearly I was going to have to solve this for them.

'Screwdriver?'

'Oooh … that's a good one. Mebbe in the cutlery drawer,' said Erna, making a beeline for the kitchen.

I switched off the computer and pulled the plug.

'Are you expecting an important email?' I asked Barbara.

'Nah, Erna's ex died. Sudden like.'

'Oh, sorry to hear it,' I said, wondering if I'd heard her right.

'Aw, don't worry about it,' shouted Erna, as she marched into the room brandishing a screwdriver. She handed it to me.

I screwed open the plug. Sure enough, one of the wires was loose. Could it really be that simple? I nudged the strand of copper back into the hole and tightened the screw, still trying to work out what the clapped-out computer had to do with Erna's dead ex.

The sisters had settled on the sofa, waiting for me to provide the visuals.

'They must be 20 minutes into it by now,' Barbara sighed. 'It's ten to bleedin' one.'

Here goes. I shoved the plug back into the socket and flicked the on switch. The computer rattled into life and the manufacturer's name popped up on the screen.

'Ha! We have liftoff,' I beamed.

'Quick, Babs, type in the www thingy,' said Erna. 'Thanks, Mr Handyman. We'll give you a shout when the coffee's ready.'

I returned to my bike, fished a piece of sandpaper from my Simson tin and rubbed it over the puncture a few times.

'Bingo!' I heard one of them exclaim. 'Oh, look, now it wants the code. Here, Babs. At the bottom of the card: Z-4-R-V-6-4-P-P.'

It all went quiet. Was the old computer already feeling the strain?

I screwed the red top off the tube of glue. The clear liquid was already oozing out.

Rubber solution. One whiff and I was back in the bushes behind my parents' house, hiding out with my pals and passing around the Simson. A couple of deep sniffs were enough to make you feel pleasantly dizzy. Heads spinning, we'd lie back on the ground, tell each other dirty stories and crease up in endless laughing fits. There was no stopping us till the tube was completely empty. We even sliced it open so not a drop of the sticky stuff would go to waste.

'Yay! It's working!' Erna yelled.

Slow, tinny music was coming from the computer's knackered speakers, sounding weirdly like a church organ with all its stops pulled out. I smeared the solution on the inner tube and the patch and blew to dry it a little before pressing the two firmly together with my thumbs. All the while, I pricked up my ears so as not to miss a word from the twins. What on earth were they watching?

'Not a bad turnout. You never can tell.'

The patch was stuck in place. I pumped a little air into the tube. No leak.

The organ music had stopped. From the living room I heard the strains of 'You'll Never Walk Alone'. Gerry and the Pacemakers.

'What moron picked that? It's what that sad old crooner Lee Towers sings once a decade when Feyenoord actually win something. Don't they know he was a Sparta supporter?'

I was beginning to tell the two voices apart. This was the pink sister. Her sentences had more of a final lilt than her red twin's.

If it was a football match, then the teams must be coming out onto the pitch. Was Erna's Sparta fan one of the players?

Time to flex my muscles and flip the last section of the tyre back onto the wheel. I pressed the lever between tyre and rim. Easy does it: punch another hole in the tube and I could start all over again. Whew. The edge of the tyre slipped neatly over the rim.

'Coffee's ready. Come and have a sit down.'

I peered around the doorpost. Barbara was pointing at the sofa, coffee pot in hand.

Erna was sitting with her legs tucked under her behind, staring unblinkingly at the screen. There wasn't much room. I tried to sit without rubbing up against her. Barbara squeezed in on the other side of me.

'Look, there's that cow of a wife of his.' Erna pointed at the screen.

'My God! Check out the dress,' Barbara tutted. 'Tits out for the lads, even on a day like this. Once a slag, always a slag.'

Peering at the screen, I saw neat rows of smartly dressed people staring solemnly into space. In the front row, a woman in a black hat was rummaging around in her handbag.

Barbara placed a friendly hand on my thigh and turned to me with a confidential air. She nodded in the direction of her sister.

'Erna's ex died last Tuesday. We got an invite with a code that lets you watch the funeral online.' She showed me the card. 'Bizarre, eh? And the mad thing is it actually works!'

The camera panned along the front row of mourners, one of whom struck a chord with Erna. 'Look at those lips! The old tart's been at the Botox again.'

She went down on her knees and leaned forwards to pour the coffee, treating me to an eyeful of cleavage. She made no effort to cover up.

'Milk? Sugar?' she asked.

'Both please,' I said.

She handed me a mug full to the brim with piping-hot coffee and disappeared into the kitchen for the rest. I blew on it gently.

Barbara began to whisper. 'Erna can't stand him now, after the fact. But he was a lovely fella. Had a go on him once or twice myself. Of course, she doesn't know that.'

I blew on my mug again. Too hard, this time. A little wave of coffee broke over the rim.

'Handyman's had an accident. Bring a cloth, will you, Erna?' Barbara yelled over her shoulder, then turned back to me, whispering. 'Gave me one of the best seeing-to's I've ever had. Got up to all sorts, we did.' She peered back at the kitchen. 'Erna, be a love and grab a pack of choccy biccies while you're at it.'

Barbara snuggled back up to me. 'He told me my sister was a right bore in bed. Never game for anything. Up, down, in, out, and that was yer lot.'

A cupboard door slammed and Erna returned with a dishcloth in one hand and a packet of biscuits in the other. She tossed the biscuits at Barbara. I resigned myself to black coffee.

The camera focused on the coffin, at the front of the chapel. A simple model, light-coloured wood.

'Nice box,' said Erna as she plumped down beside me, dishcloth in hand. 'Sooner they set light to it, the better.' She took my mug, wiped the bottom and handed it back to me. Without missing a beat she began to dab at the wet patches between my thighs.

All down my left side I could feel her heat through the pink jogging pants. The sisters' perfume was identical, overpowering with more than a hint of honeysuckle.

'Dickhead,' snapped Erna, as the camera zoomed in on the photo propped up on the coffin.

'Come off it, Erna,' Barbara tutted. 'I mean, it's not like you two didn't have some good times.'

'Yeah, till he started shagging any old slapper he could lay his hands on.'

Barbara pinched my thigh.

In the chapel, an elderly man walked up to the microphone. He was trembling and leaning on a walking stick.

'His dad,' Barbara confided in my ear.

'Jesus, the old goat's in bad shape,' said Erna.

The man spoke about the good old days. About a carefree youth. It became clear to me that he was standing by the coffin of his only child. As he said his piece, the camera showed another selection of mourners in close-up.

'My,' said Erna. 'Uncle Frank's lost a bit up top.'

'And there's that silly cow Tina,' Barbara chimed in.

'Dana's scrounged another dress from Maxie's shop by the look of her.'

The only kind word came when the cleaning lady appeared on screen.

'Two-faced gits, the lot of 'em!' Erna burst out. 'They knew my Johnny was out messing around when he should've been home with me.'

Barbara gave a conspicuous cough.

'What did your ex die of?' I asked.

'He was working down at the docks – Beatrix Harbour – when a couple of steel plates came crashing down. Didn't have a chance. Snuffed it on the spot.'

They looked back at the screen. The mourners were getting ready to pay their final respects.

'I'm gasping for a fag,' said Erna, and stormed off to the kitchen.

The coffin was rolled forwards on its bier and a door began to slide open.

'Erna! Hurry! He's goin' down the hatch.'

The funeral director called on the congregation to stand. Barbara stood up too, tugging up her jogging pants.

'Erna! Get a move on! They're getting ready to pop him in the oven.'

Erna came marching back in with an unlit cigarette dangling from her lips and stood behind me with her hands resting on the back of the sofa. She made no move to light up.

Another piece of music began to play. U2. I started poking around in my memory banks but Erna put me out of my misery.

'"I Still Haven't Found What I'm Looking For". Might have known. He used to play it full blast in the car at least twice a week. Piss-awful song.'

'Don't go getting all sentimental now,' said Barbara.

Four black-suited pallbearers went up and stood next to the coffin, two on either side. At a sign from the funeral director, they removed their hats. A brief silence followed. One of the four gave a nod. They placed their hands on the coffin handles and slid it towards the hatch.

I felt the warmth of Barbara's thigh against my skin.

Erna was still standing behind me. 'Fire up the burners!' she yelled.

Barbara's hand sought mine. She rubbed her fingers over my knuckles and I felt the scratch of her polished nails. I glanced to the side and saw that she had been crying. She continued to look straight ahead at the people on the screen, all waiting patiently for a sign that they could file out of the chapel.

The furnace door slid slowly shut.

Erna murmured something but I couldn't make out what it was.

The funeral director turned to the dearly beloved. 'Now that we have paid our last respects and said a fitting farewell to John, on behalf of the family I would like to thank you for being here today and invite you to join us for refreshments in the foyer. Our thanks also go to those of you who watched this service online.'

Erna marched over and switched off the computer. One quick flash and the screen went dark.

Barbara had slipped out of the room. I could hear the kitchen tap running.

'Well, that tyre won't pump itself up ...'

Back out in the hall, I went at it with the pump till the tyre was nice and hard. Then I decided to top up my front tyre for good measure.

Hesitantly, Barbara came into the hall and stood with her back to the wall. I squeezed the rubber again. Another few strokes should do it.

Barbara looked at my knees bending and straightening as I worked the pump. Erna came and stood beside her. For the first time, I noticed that she was a little smaller than her sister.

I was ready for the road once more. I turned the bike over and it landed a little too violently on its wheels. The bouncing back tyre left a couple of stripes on the lino.

'Thanks for the air and the coffee.'

'And thank *you*, Mr Handyman, for getting that heap of junk up and running,' Erna answered.

Barbara looked deep into my eyes, a look I couldn't fathom. Was she trying to make sure her secret was safe with me?

Outside on the mossy paving stones, I clipped my shoes into the pedals. Erna lingered in the doorway as I cycled down the path. When I turned onto the road, I saw Barbara appear at the window. Both sisters were in my view but hidden from each other.

Barbara drew something in the condensation with the tip of her finger. I made out the shape of a heart. Almost immediately, she pressed her palm to the glass and erased it with a firm swipe worthy of a windscreen wiper.

Erna was still standing in the doorway. She pulled the zip of her pink top up to her chin. I directed my wave at the corner of the house, halfway between door and window. So this is how you wave goodbye to twins, I thought. A farewell split down the middle.

Red 'n' pink. Pink 'n' red.

The bull terrier shot past Erna and charged down the road after me, barking like a thing possessed.

FRONT WHEEL SPINNING

Netherlands

Clocking a higher average speed than normal, around 33kmph, I was determined to keep my pace up. The narrow path wound its way through a stretch of parkland. Soon I'd have the wind at my back again.

A sharp bend to the left was followed immediately by a right, then up a slight incline for 50 metres or so before the path curved right again, more gently this time. I tucked in low over the bars and as I rounded the last bend I felt the descent begin. I was already flying and felt my speed increase.

A young boy was standing on the path, bike between his legs. His eyes widened when he saw me hurtling towards him and he shouted to a man at the side of the path, his father most likely.

The father waved his son over. Stupid thing to do.

'Look out!' I yelled.

The boy began to waddle across, bike still between his legs. I braked and took note of the soft clay on either side of him.

Boy and bike had come to a standstill, taking up the full width of the path.

I continued to squeeze the brakes but I was bombing down the slope at too high a speed.

Don't hit the boy! Don't hit the boy! Aim for his bike. The front wheel.

My wheel slammed into his. The impact brought my bike to a direct standstill. I shot out of my pedals, over the boy and through the air.

Behind me I heard the boy's head hit the deck. I landed at the side of the road and the momentum sent me tumbling across the clay. I looked back, dazed. The boy lay crying in the middle of the path, his bike on top of him.

The front wheel was still spinning.

* * *

THE FATHER MUST HAVE SEEN EVERYTHING. He came walking over to us. The boy was still sobbing, hands clamped to the back of his head.

'Idiot,' snarled the father.

I was just about to stammer an apology, till I realised he was talking to his son.

A fat tow-haired kid with a bright-red face, he struggled to sitting. His tears wouldn't stop.

'Calm down, calm down,' I said, a little too loudly. 'Where does it hurt?'

He continued to sob.

'Never cross over when there's a bike approaching!' the father shouted.

The son lowered his hand to reveal a sizeable bump on the back of his head.

'It's not bleeding,' I observed.

The boy sat there with his eyes closed.

'In one ear, out the other,' the man muttered, tugging at his son's arm. 'On your feet and less of your blubbering.'

I recalled the sound of his head hitting the asphalt and winced inwardly.

'What's your name?' I asked.

'Jesse,' said the boy, wiping his eyes.

'And what's your postcode?'

'3024 BM,' his father answered for him. 'There's nothing wrong with you. Now get up.'

Jesse struggled to his feet and stared down at his grazed knees.

'We got him a bike in the hope he'd lose a few pounds,' said the father. 'Fat chance!' He poked his son's waistline.

I walked over to my bike and checked to see if my rims were buckled. They seemed to be turning okay. I spotted my bottle at the edge of the bike path, almost all its contents spilled. I pushed it back in its holder.

The father examined his son's bike for damage. 'Hah! Bent wheel. That's all we need.'

He was right. The front wheel was catching. Without asking permission, I eased the tension on the brake so the pads no longer touched the rim. 'That should make things easier. Will you make it home okay?'

'Yeah, with me pushing,' said the father.

The boy stuck a finger in his mouth and rubbed some spit into the graze on his elbow. He was looking a little less dazed.

'Failing that, I'll give his mother a call. She lives not far from here.'

As I got back on my bike, I looked at the boy once more. He seemed a little calmer.

'Take it easy, okay? Have a nice bath when you get home,' I said.

Jesse wiped away the last of his tears and looked at me briefly.

My handlebars were crooked. A couple of good whacks with the palm of my hand and they were back in position.

My bike computer was still in one piece. Highest recorded speed: 49kmph. Right before impact, no doubt. I put my foot on the pedal.

'Right then, I'll be off.'

The father nodded without another word.

Moving away from the scene of the collision, I noticed that my knee was hurting. My hip joined in, followed by my elbow. My bike would be lucky to leave the shed for the next few weeks.

I cycled home at a snail's pace.

CRAMP

Netherlands

HANDS UNDER THE TABLE, I was struggling to free my fingers from my brand-new cycling gloves. I had ordered them on-line and ticked the box that said 'medium'. Three days later, a courier had delivered the parcel to my door. Soft white leather, cut-away knuckles. Tight as a second skin. They were a bastard to take off.

I slurped at the milky foam of my cappuccino without lifting the cup.

'Too hot?' asked the waitress.

'No, fine, thanks.'

She moved on to the next table. The first warm day of spring had brought the Dutch out in force and business was brisk at the pavement café in the seaside town of Noordwijk.

I finally managed to peel off my second skin and my finger was free to slip through the handle of my coffee cup. I took an impatient gulp. Coffee makes the day. Without coffee I was barely human, let alone fit to cycle.

Caffeine. Too much will get you into trouble as a rider.

Italian cyclist Gianni Bugno was once caught consuming too much caffeine. Furiously he turned on the doping inspector. 'Of course I drink lots of espresso! I'm Italian!' he fumed. 'Yes, but not a thousand cups a day,' countered the inspector with a tube of tested urine in his hand.

Bugno could count on my sympathy. Caffeine isn't doping. Coffee is part of a cyclist's standard regime. And a blessing for the bowels into the bargain. Coffee belongs in the cycling pantheon, up there with pasta, water, protein gel, isotonic drinks, muesli bars, bananas and rice cakes.

I scooped the last of the foam from my cup and gazed out over the beach. A bunch of surfers were pulling on their wetsuits. One of the lads examined the underside of his board and tossed it into the waves.

I paid for my coffee.

'Off to Scheveningen again today?' the waitress asked.

'Exactly.' I stuck a finger in the air. 'The wind will blow me there and fight me all the way back.'

• • • •

THE BOULEVARD WAS A CRUSH of cars and buses. After a 50-metre slalom, I turned right onto the bike path, the start of my route through the dunes. I shifted up to the big chainring and it took a few seconds for my legs to adjust. I got up on the pedals and hauled myself into action.

It was an ideal spring day to get aero and go full tilt. The numbers on my display were rising nicely as my tyres zipped over the worn asphalt. The speedometer settled at around 45kmph. Fast by my standards. The wind had scattered fine sand from the dunes across sections of the path. I had to be careful not to slip.

I blasted one nostril clear, then the other, and sucked in the salty air. A relief compared to the semi-smog of the city. I reckoned I was already cycling at 90 per cent of my capacity, a time triallist in a race against the clock. Scheveningen and back usually took me an hour and a half, give or take. I raised my head from its tucked position and took a look ahead. There was no one on the path. I jettisoned a gob of phlegm. Perfect. Nothing more to impede my breathing. Man as machine: an air pump, oil, a full tank, moving parts. All ticking over nicely with the wind at my back.

I was five kilometres in before I saw the first sign of life on the path. A stick-wielding little man striding stiffly towards me. Nordic walking. What evil mind had exported *that* to Holland? From senior citizen to laughing stock in one easy lesson.

The man seemed convinced I was about to run him over, tutting and shaking his head.

'Easy does it!' he blustered as I whizzed past.

'Bike path!' I yelled back.

The route began to dip and rise. My front wheel sang a little louder as the asphalt flashing past beneath me turned rougher. No need to change up a gear. With the wind at my back I could cycle on suppleness alone. It would be a while yet before the dunes dished up a more challenging climb.

I looked up and noticed I had a couple of black-headed gulls for company. They were taking it even easier than I was. The wind beneath their outstretched wings was doing all the work. Were they counting on me to toss them a crust or two, in anticipation of a summer spent feasting on the leftovers of Dutch sun-seekers?

The gulls flew so close that I could make out the movement of their black heads. Miffed that I had nothing to offer them, they veered off and flapped fiercely into the wind. That would be my fate too when I reached the water tower by Scheveningen and turned back. There are few things finer than powering through the dunes wind-assisted. I stopped pedalling for a second and shook the tension from my legs.

Next to me on the path a shadow slid into view. I recognised the shape of a helmet. Don't look back. How long had this guy been behind me? I stayed low and maintained my speed. When would he pass me? Or was he expecting a sign to take over the lead? A

Tour rider would stick an elbow out to the side, once was enough. Standard shorthand for domestiques, especially when they've been toiling away at the front to keep their sprinter within striking distance of a stage win.

If he stayed behind me, I would know he was happy to stick to my pace. I took another glance at his shadow. The shape told me this was a cyclist who knew his aerodynamics. Pros nowadays withstood wind tunnels to perfect their position. Coloured wind was blown at them as they pedalled in a sealed space and the whole thing was filmed so they could watch it back and see where the resistance built up. Perhaps they needed to tuck their arms under their chest more or dip the head a touch lower between the shoulders. Cycling as a science. I understood it, of course I did: time trials are decided on tenths of a second. Yet my heart still spoke the old-school lingo of grit, pain and perseverance.

Sharp bend coming up. I knew this route like the back of my hand. How many times had I covered it? Ideal terrain for restoring the power to your legs in the spring. Around that bend, you come face to face with a daunting dune. I tightened my grip on the handlebars to give myself better purchase on the climb.

My pace was still impressive but with the first metres of the climb behind me I had no choice but to change down a gear. My speed dropped to 30kmph. My follower was still in tow. Was he planning to stay behind me all the way up the dune?

If there's one thing I can't stand, it's a wheelsucker.

No, here he came. To my left a front wheel edged into my field of vision, first its shadow, then the wheel itself. My unknown adversary was making his move. Now came the frame. I glanced to the side and saw SPECIALIZED on a red tube. Good make.

He went past me at a cracking pace. It was all I could do not to be dropped then and there. With a few powerful thrusts of my legs I was barely able to latch on to his back wheel. A youngster. Long, tanned legs, white socks, white shoes. KATWIJK CYCLING CLUB spelled out across his shirt. Short sleeves. Smooth arms with a dusting of downy hair. Broad back, wasp waist. What age could this guy be? To find out I would have to pass him and get a good look at his face. Another 50 metres to the top of the dune. No, I had to stay put. To overtake here would be sporting suicide.

As the young rider stood on his pedals just before the top, I looked at his skinny backside suspended above the saddle. Most of the power seemed to be coming from his thighs, pumping like pistons. I gritted my teeth to match his pace. My breathing was fast, too fast, but I had to keep up. So much for suppleness – I was hanging on for grim death. My front wheel was 20 centimetres from his back wheel. Then 30. Don't give up. I switched down another gear in the hope of picking up my rhythm. It was no good. A metre opened up between us. Then two. Then three.

I had to let him go.

•　•　•

AT THE TOP OF THE DUNE I was gasping for air. My legs felt wrecked. The young rider had taken the descent without pedalling and was now a good way ahead. No time to drink in the wonderful view across the dunes this time around. I had to battle to get back into his slipstream. By the time the descent was over I was tucked in behind him again. I was still short of breath, wheezing like an engine with leaky valves.

The youngster hadn't looked back once.

I looked down. The misshapen shadow of my head was already looming beneath his pedals. He must know that I was back on his tail.

A flat stretch was coming up. This was the moment to up gear. I took a moment to spur myself on. You can do this!

I steered left and felt the full force of the wind. The youngster looked down at his pedals. He must have noticed my shadow inching forwards; a sign for him to pick up the pace. I saw the tension grip his smooth calves. I shifted up another gear and dipped as low as possible. All for nothing. My tormentor eased away from me with a supple change of rhythm.

Within seconds, the distance between us grew to 20 or 30 metres. I was powerless to stop it and it pissed me off no end. A rabbit with bald patches in its fur shot across the path and zigzagged into the dunes.

I struggled to maintain my pace. Meanwhile the youngster held his legs still. With an almighty effort I caught him again. He didn't look back and didn't give me a second's respite. As soon as he sensed my front wheel creeping close, he gave another spurt. I cursed my shadow for giving me away.

This smartarse was taking the piss. I couldn't just sit back and let him get away with it. When he took a swallow from his bottle, I seized my chance and swung out from behind him with everything I had in me. Another few strokes of the pedals and I could look him in the face, see who I was up against.

The youngster slipped his bottle back into its holder. My shoulders were rolling from side to side. Centimetre by centimetre I crawled alongside him. Just a few more turns of the crank.

At last I pulled level. He looked to the side with a soft smile. The face of a teenager, blue eyes, fleshy lips, flushed cheeks.

'Hi,' I said.

He nodded in reply.

'Scheveningen?' I panted.

'Yeah. There and back. Nice training run. You heading that way too?'

He had braces on his teeth and the words hissed moistly from his mouth.

I nodded and spat in tandem. 'Fast,' I panted paternally. 'You.'

'Not bad yourself, mister.'

Mister. Be polite to your elders.

'How old … are you?'

'Fifteen.'

'Really?'

'Yeah, people always think I'm older cos I'm big for my age. Heavy too. I could do with losing another kilo.'

His legs seemed to be on automatic. He was cycling at a furious rate. I looked at my speedometer and saw 51kmph. I had never cycled this fast in my life against the clock.

'Done much cycling?' I enquired.

'Around 20,000k a year.'

I thought of the measly 3,000 I had managed to clock up at the end of last year.

'I'm club champion. Just the juniors, like.'

'Good going.'

Another steep dune was looming. I took a deep breath and pointed.

'Be my guest,' said the kid.

Heaving myself up on the pedals, I overtook him. The chit-chat had left me even more winded. Back on the saddle. Settle your breathing. Nose in, mouth out. No use. I was chasing my breath.

The climb began and I battled against my plummeting pace. Why should I give up? Just because he's younger? Age isn't everything. At 40, German rider Jens Voigt was still a fanatical member of many a leading group. A body immune to wear and tear. Fathered six kids along the way, scuppering the theory that too much cycling puts your balls out of commission. My breathing was still hurried and ragged but I wasn't worried. Now and then it can be a thrill to ignore your body's cries for help. I wasn't one of the new breed who fly into a panic as soon as their heart-rate monitor hits red.

Red is the zone where the real battle starts. Red separates the men from the boys. The zone where an athlete's heart is born.

I looked left, right. The boy's shadow was nowhere to be seen. I looked back to see him trailing by 20 metres, cycling with his hands on the tops. Had he run out of steam? Ha! What did I tell you? Age, kilometres in training: it says nothing about inner strength. In cycling, it all comes down to grit, guts and sheer bloody-mindedness.

Another 100 metres to the crest of the dune. I pictured myself sitting tall on the saddle, straightening up my shirt and extending both hands to the blades of long grass, as if to acknowledge a thousand cheering fans.

Over my shoulder came the hum of tyres. Before I could even look, the kid had zoomed past me. Up on his pedals, pushing a high gear. Powerful strokes. With every rotation he left me a few metres further behind.

I stood out of the saddle. Thrust, two, three, four. He didn't seem to be getting any further away. Hang on in there! My lungs squeaked in protest again as I nudged a little closer.

Pain skewered my right calf. As if the muscle was being sucked out by force. Cursing and swearing, I stalled on my pedals. The kid was rocking his bike gently to and fro. In that same relaxed cadence he steadily stretched his lead.

I got back up on my pedals but as soon as I put my foot down, the pain struck again. Thrusting hard with my left leg to maintain some kind of momentum, I freed my right foot from the pedal and sank back onto the saddle in an effort to shake the cramp.

Heel down, toes up. It had little effect. My bike swerved to the left.

Nothing else for it. I extricated my other foot, braked and ground to a halt on the sandy verge.

As I pressed my thumb hard into the knot in my calf, I looked up. Of course, the kid had already reached the dune top. He sat down on his saddle and disappeared from view.

Egotistical little git.

I stood there, panting, hunched over the handlebars. Too tired to pick up my bottle, I staggered a little further from the path. Utterly defeated, I stared into space. Some distance away, two ladies in shorts came strolling through the dunes. Was one of them peering at me through her binoculars? I straightened my backbone. The other woman pointed. Not at me, but at the dune behind me. I looked around and saw a pheasant dash for the cover of some thick bushes, half flapping, half running.

There was little point in picking up where I'd left off. My right calf was stiff with lactic acid and the knot would only return. My legs felt too heavy to lift. Lead weights encased in concrete.

I creaked onto the saddle and freewheeled back down the dune. As soon as I reached the flat, I took a right at a little white marker that read BEACH 0.5KM and headed for a spot where I had taken a breather on a previous outing. The wind grew cooler and when I came to a rise in the path, I knew the sea lay just beyond. As a child, the first sight of that strip of blue emerging from among the dunes had always been a magical moment. Now I was too whacked for enchantment.

Where the path met the beach, I dismounted and leaned my bike against a bin. I lowered myself onto a bench and buried my head in my hands. Empty shells dotted the sand at my feet.

Slowly, I straightened up. At full stretch I could just reach my bottle in its holder. I gulped down its entire contents while the sun warmed my legs. I massaged my calves. They were already becoming more pliable.

A whiff of deep fat fryer wafted towards me. Only now did I notice a wooden cabin selling fish. An elderly couple were waiting for their order, e-bikes at their side. I waited till they had sauntered off before staggering up to the shack. The owner was standing with his back to me, stirring the oil with an oversized straining spoon.

Fatty food and serious cycling: not a match made in heaven. I was determined to be in peak condition that summer when I set out to tackle the mountains of France and Italy. But here I was, face to face with a tray of raw herring. Heads chopped off, neatly gutted, skin glistening. A Dutchman's definition of mouth-watering, take my word for it.

The owner tossed a portion of fried fish into a draining dish and turned to greet me.

'What can I do for you, sir?' he said in a thick Hague accent.

'One herring roll.'

'Coming right up.'

He sliced open a soft white roll, buttered both sides with a spoon and placed a herring in the middle. Juicy, reddish-brown flesh.

'Onions?'

'Please.'

'Pickled gherkin?'

'No thanks.' By which I meant not on your life.

The man put a paper napkin on the counter and placed the roll on top. 'Something to wash it down?'

Water was the word on the tip of my tongue. Water, water, always water. Only now my body was crying out for a sugar rush.

'Give me a Coke,' I said.

The man put a can down next to the roll. It hissed seductively as I opened it. I took a few grateful gulps.

'You look shattered, mate.'

Right on cue, my cough began to play up again. I cleared my throat. 'Yeah, I've had quite a session.' I spat a gob of phlegm off to the side of his shack.

'Don't mind me,' said the man, raising his eyebrows. He took a dripping dishcloth from a mayonnaise bucket and began wiping down his fryer.

I took a greedy bite of bread, butter, salted fish and raw onion.

'Don't often see a cyclist tucking into a herring roll,' he remarked, wringing out his cloth.

'Too fatty,' I said.

The shack owner lifted his oil-spattered shirt and gave his gut an affectionate pat. 'Fat is food for the brain. I'm living proof.'

'But too much isn't good for you,' I said.

'Let's face it, mate, what *is* good for you? I'm 64. Drink what I like, eat what I like and I'm still fit as a fiddle.'

I swallowed down the last of my roll.

'What about sport?' I asked.

'An arse is for sitting on.'

The can of Coke was still half full. 'What do I owe you?'

'That'll be six euros.'

He took my tenner, rummaged around behind the counter and gave me four change.

'Just a mo'.' He filled a plastic tray with chunks of fried fish and dolloped the sidecar full of tartare sauce.

'On the house. You look like you could use it.'

I gave another deep cough and felt the air catch in my windpipe. 'Thanks. Don't mind if I do.'

I dipped a warm chunk of battered fish in the sauce and put it in my mouth. Why did I always have to bang on about the evils of fat?

'Enjoy life while you can,' said the man. 'That's what I say.'

The can was still on the counter. I screwed open my empty water bottle and poured in what was left of the Coke.

SAND WAS BLASTING my face as I set off along the bike path back to Noordwijk. Scheveningen was a bridge too far today. I sat a little taller on the saddle to give myself more room to breathe. My calves were crying out for a velvet cushion.

Another 20 kilometres to go. Climbing the first dune I had to resort to gears I'd normally only use on a tough alpine climb. I checked my speed and hung my head in shame.

In an act of desperation, I downshifted again. Every little helps. I began to consider getting off and pushing the bike up the hill. All enjoyment was gone. The tang of the sauce filled my mouth again. I took a swig of Coke from my bottle but the taste remained. A nasty shade of sour.

From behind came the clicking of gears and before I could turn my head I felt a broad hand on my back.

'Stay on the saddle!'

I looked over my shoulder. Katwijk Cycling Club's junior champ was back to haunt me. My speedometer zoomed up from 15 to 25kmph. 'No need,' I shouted.

One look at my face was enough to tell him I was lying.

His legs pumped away as he pushed. My weight barely seemed to register with him. I was pedalling in thin air, a toddler on a kiddie bike being propelled along by dad.

The top of the dune came into view.

'Sorry,' I muttered.

'No problem. I can use the extra power training.'

Being pushed up a climb that should have been a doddle. Helpless, hopeless. So this was how it felt to be an old codger in a wheelchair.

The Tour de France strictly forbids riders to accept a helping hand. Yet on punishing mountain stages it happens anyway. Riders plead with their eyes – *poussez!* – but have to tell fans off for breaking the rules as soon as they pitch in. Official cars and jury members are never far away.

We came over the brow of the dune. In the distance I could make out the buildings of Katwijk. I drew level with the boy.

'Thanks,' I said.

He nodded. I was nothing to him. Dead weight he could train with. A man of 70 kilos had been used to pump up the thighs of a fresh-faced kid. Katwijk's boy wonder pressed a button on his bike computer. 'Average wattage 340, heart rate 140. Awesome.' I shrugged. Watts were for lightbulb salesmen. We rode down the dune, side by side. The boy shook his thighs loose.

'You okay?' he asked.

'I'll manage.'

He pulled out a gel pack, tore it open with his teeth and squirted the contents into his mouth. He seemed to have enough in the tank for Katwijk to Scheveningen ten times over. The empty pack disappeared into his back pocket.

The boy picked up speed again. I tried to look as relaxed as possible as I set off in pursuit. Without subterfuge you won't get far as a cyclist. Keep your cards close to your chest.

Junior was in the mood for a chat. 'My stepdad puts together my training schedule. He's as fanatical as they come. We always cycle together, but he's down with the flu.'

I nodded. 'Planning to make a career of it?'

'I hope so.'

My calf was nagging again. Cramp was just around the corner.

'What's your dream race?'

'One day I'd like to win the Tour of Flanders.'

'Good choice. My favourite too.'

'Only I'm not allowed to cycle on a Sunday. We're Dutch Reformed. Where you heading?'

'Noordwijk.'

'Oh, not far to go. Another six kilometres. I'm cutting through the dunes here. Dirt track to Katwijk. Power my way home.'

The boy steered right, upped his gear and began to pound at the pedals.

'Work that body!' I called after him.

He sprinted onto the steep shell path and disappeared from view for the third time that day.

Alone again with the wind in my face, my pace slackened something awful … 25 … 22. Below 20 I began to curse the state I was in. Then came 19. I put up a fight and hit 21, for a minute or two. Then the meter began to fall … 19 again. Battling against the wind, I began to swerve across the path. A group of cyclists whizzed by me.

Noordwijk. Six kilometres felt like 60. I took a swig from my bottle and was startled by the taste of The Real Thing. Was all this sugar doing me any good? Every turn of the pedals was a drain. I began to drift again. A cyclist coming the other way had to swerve off the path to avoid a collision.

'Dickhead!' he yelled.

I raised an apologetic hand, made a conscious effort to keep right and took another swig. There was that shortness of breath again. A long, loud burp erupted from within. A filthy cocktail of fish and Coke with a dollop of sauce.

A short way before the main Katwijk turn-off, there was another high dune to tackle … 19kmph … 18 … 17. I hoisted myself off the saddle to push down on the pedals. With no strength left in my muscles, it was all down to my body weight.

I gritted my teeth and the top of the dune came closer. My mouth turned sour. I applied more force, leaning my body over the handlebars, and was rewarded with another stab in the calf. This must be a hideous spectacle. Pros dance their way up an incline, this was a drunken lurch.

My front wheel swung off the path and my right foot landed in a soft layer of drifting sand. I pulled my other shoe loose to stop myself falling and sighed to a standstill. Once again I swallowed hard.

The sting of acid.

My insides began to heave. I hung over my handlebars, mouth gaping. Before I knew it, I was staring down at a mess of herring and fried fish in a brown puddle of cola.

Shivering, I straightened up. Another surge from my midriff. Another wave, less of it this time. The acid burned my gullet and throat.

I felt completely hollow but a little more human too.

Above the dune, gulls were floating on the wind. They hung almost still in the air. Did their satanic squawking signal an appetite for chucked-up fish?

The top was closer than I thought. I pushed the bike uphill and climbed back on. The wind was so strong I had to keep pedalling on the way down. I managed it, in my lowest gear.

Passing the WELCOME TO NOORDWIJK sign, I wiped a hand across my face and rode out of the dunes and onto the boulevard in slow motion. I had made it. Clipping my shoes out of the pedals took a superhuman effort. Cycling at walking pace, I shook one leg loose, then the other. They still felt stiff.

Before long I arrived back at my regular café. I got off and parked my bike against the see-through screen. I found a corner table out of the wind, took off my helmet and heaved a sigh. I couldn't summon the energy for another wrestling match with my tight new gloves.

The sea had grown choppier, white crests had appeared on the waves. Surfers were expertly manoeuvring their way ashore, jumping off their boards at the very last minute.

The waitress caught my eye and made a cheery beeline for my table.

'Apple pie and cappuccino?' she asked.

'Just water please.'

She eyed me suspiciously.

'Nothing to eat today?'

'No, water's fine. Really.'

'Water. Okay, suit yourself.' She stalked off to the bar.

Two surfers parked their boards next to my bike and sat down at a table. They opened their wetsuits to the waist. Shaved chests. One of them had worked hard for a six-pack. They gave me a friendly nod.

I zipped my cycling shirt up to my chin.

'Your water,' said the waitress, barely stopping on her way over to take the surfers' order.

As I took a sip, I saw the acid had eaten away at my brand-new gloves. I rubbed the marks with my thumb. No use.

From now on I'd be riding with yellow stains on my soft white leather.

A PULSE OF 48

Netherlands

MY GP SLID THE BLACK BAND UP MY ARM, popped the ends of his stethoscope in his ears and pressed the cold disc gently to the swollen vein.

'Sit still,' he said, squeezing a little rubber bulb to pump the armband tight.

What was I doing here? It's not like there was anything wrong with me. The last time I'd had a check-up, my blood pressure was fine. Then again, that had been 12 years ago.

Slowly the doctor released the air. The blood pounded in my constricted arm.

'It's 135 over 85. Very nice indeed,' he said, pulling the armband loose.

A surge of relief. At my age, high blood pressure could be a hidden assassin.

The doctor took a listen to my heartbeat.

'At rest I have a pulse of 48,' I volunteered.

'Just keep quiet a moment,' the doctor said.

A pulse at rest. It's something cyclists like to brag about. Five-time Tour winner Miguel Indurain had a heart rate of only 28 beats per minute. Powerful thuds. The Spaniard's bed shook each time his heart sent blood racing around his body.

'Your heart sounds fine,' said the doctor. 'Strong.'

'Sometimes, especially when I'm lying in bed at night, I worry it might stop any second.' There, I'd said it.

The doctor gave me a condescending smile. 'I've treated some very old patients in my time. People with all kinds of ailments. The kind that had me thinking, how long have they got? But the heart just wouldn't give up. It's made to keep beating.'

I rolled down my shirt sleeve. Good news. There was no assassin lurking within. I could go on cycling to my heart's content.

Back at home, I chomped down a few slices of bread and jam, pulled on my cycling gear and headed out on my run along the River Rotte.

Cycling a couple of metres below sea level, I climbed the steepest section of a hill that barely deserved the name. In my youth, tons of slurry from the harbour had been dumped on this low-lying polder within striking distance of Rotterdam. There was every chance the asphalt beneath my spinning wheels covered dark sludge from the bed of what was now the Nieuwe Waterweg canal.

I stood out of the saddle and felt my thighs burn. Head pounding, breathing fast, chest tight. No harm in a little pain, as long as you know you're healthy.

The summit of Slurry Hill was already approaching.

As I sped down the short descent, a helicopter flew over, lower than usual. For a Tour rider, the sound of the rotors means one thing: a live broadcast. But I'm no pro. My first thought was an accident, a trauma in *ER*-speak. No danger of me being wheeled in on a stretcher though. Here I was, healthy and relaxed on the saddle, enjoying my newly confirmed low blood pressure.

The helicopter came in to land on the other side of the hill. A siren sounded in the distance.

I decided to double back and head up the slope in the opposite direction. When I reached the top, I saw the helicopter in the middle of a field a short distance away. I knew the place well. Beyond it lay a path along the Rotte I had cycled ever since I can remember.

Continuing my route, I approached the scene of the calamity. Not far from the helicopter, by the kitchen garden of a detached house, stood an ambulance, lights flashing. With around 100 metres to go, I slowed down and unclipped my shoes.

I could only see the backs of the ambulance personnel as they leaned over someone or something. A couple of men were screening off the garden with a sheet of orange plastic. That's when you know it's serious.

After five minutes I'd had enough of being a voyeur and set off down a road that ran parallel to the bike path. Looking over, I noticed a girl on a racing bike leaving the spot where the ambulance was parked. She must have seen what had happened by the garden.

I crossed a little bridge that led me onto the bike path. The girl was ahead of me, cracking along at a decent pace. I had to work hard to catch her. Just as I was about to pull level, she braked to look at a map at the side of the path. I joined her.

"Scuse me, but weren't you just at the scene of that accident?' I asked. 'What was up?'

A robust girl, chunky thighs and rosy cheeks.

'Man out for a cycle. Collapsed into the bushes, bike and all. Heart attack, I think.'

For a moment there was nothing to say.

'How old was he?'

'Must've been around 50.'

'Is he going to make it, d'you think?'

Her face clouded over and she shook her head gently.

'I was one of the first on the scene. A couple of other cyclists were already pounding away at his chest. He was foaming at the mouth. I don't think he'll make it. Ambulance was a long time coming. It was hard to explain where we were.'

A cloud slid in front of the sun and I felt the temperature drop a few degrees. The girl traced her finger across the map.

'Where are you headed?' I asked.

'I'm looking for my dad. He was there too, but he took off down the road to show the ambulance the way. I'm not sure where he is now.'

I handed her my phone so she could call him. He picked up and they agreed to meet near the A12.

'This sport is not without its risks,' I said. 'I had my blood pressure checked only this morning. At my age you never can tell.'

Her young face looked at me. A world of difference, in age, in mindset.

'Anyway, better not keep my dad waiting. Thanks for letting me use your mobile.'

'Okay. *Ciao*,' I said.

I did an about-turn and headed back over the bike path. A few hundred metres and I would be back at the scene. Something in me wanted to see the cold hard truth that had caught up with an unsuspecting cyclist.

The ambulance was parked in the middle of the path. Riding cautiously over the verge, I ventured a look to the side. A man in a battered old cycling helmet was peering over the top of the improvised screen he was holding up. The orange plastic was flapping against his unshaven legs. The victim was well out of sight.

I fixed my gaze on the horizon. There were enough prying eyes around. A hip, heavily made-up young girl was perched on her Vespa, taking a few snaps on her iPhone.

Not many cyclists out today. Ahead lay a five-kilometre stretch of uninterrupted bike path before I had to brake to cross a busy road.

I took a swallow from my bottle, put it back in its holder and began to cycle like a man possessed. The reading on my display shot up with every turn of the pedals. I was craving speed. Faster, faster still. Flying in the face of fate.

To make up for the heart that had let somebody down, another had to race along the Rotte, pounding all the way to the finish. This heart of mine was going to make it.

It was made to keep beating.

JIM SHINE FINE

Belgium

I<small>T WASN'T HIS DAY</small>. Jim was straggling well behind the peloton and above his head a storm was building. Steady rain, no let-up, for hours on end. The entire race had been a battle not to be left behind. The pulse of each acceleration reached the last riders in the peloton with a 30-second delay. Jim's leading rider was up front, exactly where he needed to be. When they had taken that hill a while back, Jim had spotted him off in the distance. The blue shirt with the sponsor's yellow letters – SHINE FINE – was right there in the vanguard.

Jim could not be faulted. As a domestique, he had done his bit for the team. Now it was simply a matter of finishing the race and heading for the riders' hotel.

For an April day, the cold was bitter. Around 100 men had lined up in Remouchamps that morning on the first leg of a three-day race through the Ardennes region of Wallonia.

Jim heard a high-pitched whistle. Coming up from behind, a fellow straggler went past him, a young rider from Coco Bello. An Italian team backed by a wholesaler in coconut milk. Jim tried to hang on to the lad's back wheel but in vain. He gritted his teeth and watched as the Italian's powerful calves – nicely tanned for this time of year – pulled him slowly but surely out of sight.

Cars behind Jim began to blow their horns. They roared past him with one wheel in the verge. He took a look at his bike computer. Around 50 kilometres to the finish. He straightened up in the saddle. Nothing but empty road behind him. Not a bike to be seen. The team leaders' cars had all just passed him. He must be one of the last riders. The sag wagon couldn't be far behind.

·   ·   ·

MINUTES AGO, HE HAD BEEN IN THE THICK OF IT, jostling with riders and taking in the boisterous banter at the tail-end of the peloton. Now all Jim could hear was the rain, the whoosh of his tyres on wet asphalt, the sound of his own breathing, shallow and uneasy.

He looked over his shoulder. A beam of yellow light was approaching in the distance. Judging by the speed it must be a motorbike, perhaps one of the lads with spare wheels. With any luck he could hitch a sly lift. There was nothing more to cycle for and no race officials lurking this far back. Jim reduced his speed and tracked the beam as it moved closer. There was only one man in the saddle. Head to toe in black leather and wearing a helmet with a deep-purple visor.

Jim hoisted himself out of the saddle and picked up his speed. The biker was now 50 metres behind him. Jim upped his pace another notch in the hope of hanging on to the back wheel when the motorbike drew level.

The biker roared past him without so much as a look.

'Hey!' Jim yelled. 'He-ee-ee-y!'

The biker braked briefly and the red tail-light reflected on the road. As Jim struggled to catch up, he saw the biker look in his rear-view mirror. Good, Jim thought, he's got the idea. Drafting. As Jim's front wheel came within a few metres of the motorbike, the biker eased away again and Jim had to give everything to stay in the slipstream. Let himself be carried along and he might even be able to hook up with the peloton again.

The rain was streaming across the asphalt and the motorbike's back wheel sent water spraying high into the air. Riding in a shower of dirty droplets, Jim tried to concentrate on the tail-light.

The motorbike leaned to the side and took a sharp bend to the right. Jim's front wheel almost went into the verge. A split-second adjustment was the only thing that kept him from falling. The biker increased his speed and a road sign flashed past. BOMAL 15KM.

Jim glanced down and saw that they were doing 60. It dawned on him that he'd placed all his trust in this stranger to guide him over the wet road through the wind and driving rain. They must be riding close to the heart of the storm. He straightened up for a moment in the hope of catching a glimpse of the peloton or the team leaders' cars up ahead. But Jim saw nothing. The rain stung his face. He narrowed his eyes and settled low over the bars.

Despite the wet and cold, he felt his mood brighten. If they kept up this speed, there was every chance he would at least connect with a bunch of stragglers and they could soldier on at a steady pace to the finish in Malhay. The motorbike slowed and rounded a wide bend to the left. Jim lost a few metres and for a while he found himself drifting to the outside of the spraying back wheel. He could just make out the contours of the hills in the fading light and calculated that he must be around 40 kilometres from the finish. Here the road narrowed and loose stones flew up here and there. Jim braked, though his pads had little purchase on the slippery rims.

The brake light of the motorbike flared fiercely. The biker took a right, heading off the road and up a dirt track. He looked in his mirror, blew his horn twice and raised his hand briefly.

Jim braked and skidded to a halt in the gravel at the side of the road. Dazed, he began to wave back as he watched the motorbike disappear into a bank of dark trees.

'Shit! Shiiiit!'

He looked at his watch. Ten to five. His socks were soaking in his shoes. He had to get out of here. New storm clouds were gathering. How far off course was he? Jim felt like he had lost all sense of direction. He pushed off and rolled slowly down the slope ahead, barely pedalling. The sodden landscape seemed dark and dead. Like there was no human life for miles around.

Jim felt in his back pocket and found a muesli bar and a gel pack. He sucked the pack dry and tossed it in the ditch at the side of the road. Through the murk he spotted a light a little way off. Before long, a gravel driveway trailed off to his right. A farmhouse.

In this filthy weather he couldn't summon the will to retrace his route in the dark. He cycled up to the farmhouse in slow motion, leaned his bike against a fence post and walked up to the front door.

THROUGH A SMALL OVAL WINDOW JIM SAW a bare light bulb shining in the hall. His legs were stiff from the cold. Hesitantly, he rang the doorbell.

A lamp on the wall above the door flickered on. He blinked and the face of a girl appeared at the little window. She couldn't have been more than 18. As soon as their eyes met, she ducked out of sight.

'Hello?' Jim ventured.

He heard the girl dash off down the hall. Nose pressed to the glass, he knocked the door. No response. With his helmet and his mud-spattered face he must look a bit of a sight.

Jim made his way along the front of the house. Peering through a window, he saw the girl standing in the dim sitting room, her back against the door.

He hesitated again. A knock on the window would give her the fright of her life. Perhaps whistling might be less threatening. Just as he was about to purse his lips, a cat leapt up onto the table and began to hiss at him. The girl stared at the cat, raised her eyes and saw Jim standing there. Her face rigid with fear, she clasped her hand to her mouth, took two steps towards the window and then backed away again. Jim looked at her. She was wearing no make-up and everything about her face seemed larger than life. Thick eyebrows, dark staring eyes and a wide mouth.

The cat hissed again.

Jim made an apologetic, almost soothing gesture. It seemed to work. The girl grew visibly calmer. Jim took off his helmet and wiped his hand over his face and through his hair. An automatic reflex, as if he had just crossed the finish line.

He pointed towards the front door. The girl's expression still betrayed doubt, even fear, yet she gestured to Jim to make his way back to the door.

The key turned in the lock. There she stood, a sturdier figure than he had first taken her for. 'Listen, I don't know who you are or what you want but in these parts it's not normal to go ringing people's doorbell after dark. And what do those words on your shirt mean?'

Jim was taken aback by her newfound self-assurance.

'Uh, it's a brand of shoe polish. One of those bottles with a sponge on top. The polish comes out of a little hole in the sponge and ...'

'Is that your sponsor or something?'

'Yeah, I got left behind. The peloton was going too fast for me. We were heading for the finish in ...'

' ... Malhay, I know. It was in the paper. One of the Ardennes classics. Comes by here every year. My dad's a cycling fanatic. Stuck in front of the telly most weekends watching every race. Since Mum died, there's been no one to nag him about it.'

Jim was still standing out in the rain.

'I have to get to the finish. I was following a motorbike and then ...'

'But Malhay's a good 60 kilometres from here.'

'Sixty? Oh, I thought I was more like 40. I must have taken a wrong turn.'

Jim pulled up the zip of his jacket and blew a drop of water from his nose.

'Come in out of the rain for a bit,' the girl said, and opened the creaky door a little wider.

Jim took a swift glance over his shoulder to check his bike was safe where he had left it and stepped stiffly inside. His cycling gear began to drip on the granite floor in the hall.

There was a slightly sour smell in the house. He followed the girl inside and couldn't help but admire the curve of her behind, clearly visible under the rough material of her dress. She had thick socks on her feet. Jim suspected it was one of those farms where everyone still wore clogs.

THEY STOOD IN THE KITCHEN. The cat jumped onto a stool and thrust its bushy tail straight in the air.

'Mara! That's enough!' the girl shouted.

She took a towel from a hook and tossed it over to Jim.

'Tea?'

She put a kettle on the cooker, lit the gas and sat down across the kitchen table from Jim. She kept rubbing one sock against the other, as if trying to warm her feet. As she stroked the cat, it lowered its tail and a gentle purring began to emanate from its small body. All the while, the branch of a tree was tapping against the side window.

Jim broke the silence. 'You're a bit off the beaten track here. What do you do for shopping 'n' that?'

'Weshun's only four kilometres down the road,' she said, tickling the cat non-stop. 'They've got just about everything we need.'

On the kitchen table there was a pile of old local newspapers and a farming magazine. A proud farmer and his state-of-the-art milking machine adorned the cover.

'What kind of farm is this anyway?' Jim asked, a little embarrassed by his lack of rural small talk.

'We've got a barn with 100 cows out back and a cheese dairy right behind the kitchen.'

Jim had found an explanation for the sour smell he'd noticed as he came in.

The girl walked over to the sink and lifted up a tea towel to reveal half a wheel of cheese. She picked up a big curved blade with a wooden handle at either end and let it sink into the cheese, then cut off a couple of decent-sized chunks and put them on a plate. 'Here. Have a taste. It's our mature cheese.'

Jim took one bite, then another. Only now did it dawn on him how hungry he was after a day battling through the wind and rain. His last musette bag had been two hours ago: a couple of bars, some gel packs, a protein drink and a water bottle full of tepid tea. He had wolfed down almost all of it, but the boost it gave him had long since ebbed away.

As the girl made tea, the cat leapt from its stool, slunk over and pushed its head hard against Jim's bare calves. He stroked the animal's back and when that seemed to work, he tried the girl's trick of tickling it under the chin with his knuckles. Its gentle purring grew louder.

'Shine Fine … Stupid name. Do they pay well?'

'Nah, not really. But then I'm not a pro. I ride with the amateurs. Decent beer money but that's about it.' He took a cautious sip of his hot tea. 'And you?'

'What about me?'

'Still at school 'n' that?'

'Nah. Left six months ago. I'm going to stay and work on the farm with my dad. Not much else to do around here.'

The girl stared into space.

'Mind if I use your toilet?'

Absently the girl pointed to a door in the corner of the kitchen.

In the toilet, Jim hooked the latch and fumbled numbly at the leg of his cycling shorts. The cold had cut deep and it took a while for his bladder to respond. From the other side of the door he heard the clatter of a pan lid. Strange how the shivers only came once you'd been sitting still in the warm for a while, the same way frozen fingers only start to tingle when they heat up. A shudder ran through his body and a splash of piss hit the wooden toilet seat. 'Bugger,' he muttered, and did his best to mop up the damage with a wad of toilet paper before returning to the kitchen.

The girl was standing at the cooker stirring in a pan. She turned around. 'This storm's not letting up any time soon. Why don't you take a bath and I'll make you some soup?'

'There's no need, honest. It's bound to clear before long. And I don't know if your parents, er ... I mean your dad would approve.'

The girl lowered the gas under the pan and wiped her hands on her dress. 'Dad's gone to visit family in Brussels this weekend. He won't be back till tomorrow. Come on, I'll show you where everything is.'

In the hall, she pushed open the second door on the right to reveal the bathroom. She turned the two big taps on full and bent over to put the black plug in the hole. 'There you go. Soap's here. Towels are on the shelf. The green one's a good size.'

She shut the door behind her.

Jim looked in the mirror and saw that his face was streaked black and the corners of his eyes were crusted with dirt. He looked like he had just crawled out of a mine shaft. No wonder the girl had panicked. She had looked into the eyes of a swamp creature.

By now, the race was a lost cause. He would explain everything to his team leader in the morning. Jim struggled out of his wet shirt and peeled off his cycling shorts to expose the only clean skin on his body. He stepped into the bath and slowly lowered himself into the water. The first real warmth he had felt all day.

The bathroom door edged open and the girl's hand appeared holding a folded square of blue textile.

'Here. One of my dad's overalls. It should just about fit you. Put it on when you're finished. You'll catch your death in that wet cycling gear.'

She let the blue overalls fall to the floor and chucked in a pair of rubber boots for good measure.

* * *

JIM COULD SMELL THE SOUP as soon as he opened the bathroom door. He was naked under the blue overalls, the press studs fastened up to his neck. The girl was waiting for him at the kitchen table, with the cat on her lap.

'I hope vegetable soup's okay. There you go. And here's some bread to go with it.'

'Great. Thanks. Beats the riders' hotel any day. Those poor sods in Malhay will be boxed up in tiny rooms with nothing to eat but the same pasta and sauce they've had all month. Did you make it yourself?'

The girl nodded and walked over to the cupboard. She returned with a bottle of wine and two glasses. 'Want some? Dad always has a glass of wine with his dinner. Says it's good for the circulation.'

Jim nodded.

'What's your name?' he asked with his mouth full.

'Michelle.'

'I'm Jim.'

'Jim Shine Fine,' she said, taking a sip from her glass.

'Sure, I'll answer to that.'

'What's so great about this cycling lark, then? Stuck on a narrow saddle all day, balancing on those thin tyres, always the risk of a fall. Not to mention the cold.'

'Oh, it's not so bad,' said Jim, looking down at his bowl. The storm was howling around the house.

'I remember Liège–Bastogne–Liège one year,' he recalled between mouthfuls. 'Must've been 1980. Bernard Hinault won. It was freezing then too. Hardly any of the riders made it to the finish. Most of them gave up along the way. Hinault couldn't even cheer when he crossed the line. Chilled to the bone, he was. Ever heard of him? Hinault? I guess not.'

The girl shook her head and tucked her legs up under her. The wine had brought some colour to her cheeks and she was beginning to resemble a classic farm girl. The cat lay purring between them on the wicker seat of a kitchen chair.

An Irish rider in Jim's team used to shove a pencil up his cat's arse. Claimed the animal couldn't get enough of it. Jim decided to keep that anecdote to himself. When the cat stretched and jumped onto his lap, he couldn't help looking at the little red hole under its tail. Could you really get a pencil up there? He found himself weighing up the options: the point or the end with the rubber on top?

Jim stroked the length of the cat's tail. He held it tight, teasing till the cat had had enough and lashed out with its front paw, leaving a couple of scratches on his hand.

Michelle gave the animal a slap. 'Mara! Bad!'

It slouched off and disappeared under the kitchen cupboard, eyes lighting up in the dark.

When Jim turned his gaze back, he saw Michelle staring at him with her chin resting in her hands. She brushed her hair behind her ears, looked at the clock above Jim's head and smiled.

Jim looked over his shoulder. Nine o'clock.

'Late for a cyclist, I bet,' Michelle frowned. 'Aren't you supposed to get lots of sleep?'

'Oh, they're not that strict. I'm only a domestique. Nobody's too bothered what I do.'

Jim saw himself back at the start in Remouchamps, surrounded by his teammates. The locals had lined the quayside, ready to cheer the peloton on its way. One and a half kilometres later the riders were already battling their way up Côte de La Redoute, a merciless climb.

'Anyway, I'd better get to bed myself,' Michelle went on. 'Have to get up at half-five to see to the cows. Are you still planning to head on to the finish?'

'No. I'd rather stay here. If it's all right with you. '

'Yeah, that's okay,' said Michelle. She rinsed his empty glass and turned out the light. Now there was only the outside lamp shining in through the window to see by.

They went into the hall and climbed the wooden stairs. Jim could see Michelle's thighs peeping out from under her dress. Beautiful, milk-white flesh. She walked across the landing and pushed open a door at the far end. As Jim admired the paintwork, the cat shot past them.

'This is the spare room,' she said as she entered. 'There's a wash-hand basin and I've left towels on the chair. Night then.' As Michelle left the room, the cat slipped out between her legs.

Jim closed the curtains and crawled into bed without taking off his overalls. It took a while for his body heat to dispel the cold between the sheets. The light on the landing went out. He felt odd, lying here in this strange house, in a strange bed, with a strange girl in another bed only metres away. Here he lay in the dark, an amateur cyclist, a city boy in a remote farmhouse. He could just go to sleep, of course he could. But instead he got out of bed and began to feel his way across the landing.

. . .

THE NEXT MORNING JIM WOKE with a start at the sound of a gate being opened. The rattle of the metal took a while to die away. Jim kept his eyes shut. He needed a moment to work out where he was.

He glanced at his watch. Half-nine. He remembered his blind search for the girl's room, Michelle – yes, that was her name – his feet shuffling across the floorboards, his fingertips gliding along walls and doorposts.

He took another look at his watch. Yes, it really was half past nine in the morning. He heard a car drive into the farmyard. The engine was turned off, a door slammed, then came the sound of footsteps.

Jim had homed in on Michelle's breathing. Slow and deep, a little catch in her throat at the end of each breath. He walked around her bed, one foot in front of the other, the same three-quarter bed as in the spare room. Her breathing remained calm and peaceful as he lifted the bedclothes and slid into bed beside her.

The sheets felt warm. She must have moved in her sleep. His feet encountered a weight on the bed. He pushed his toes against it through the bedclothes and heard the cat jump onto the floor. Jim eased over until he felt the warmth of Michelle's skin through his overalls. His front touching her back. Overalls and a night-dress. A cyclist and a farm girl.

He hadn't been fazed by the shrill cry she'd let out when he put his hand around her waist. No, that would pass. She had been more than kind to him these past few hours. Surely a man's allowed to read something into an invitation to stay the night?

Outside, the sound of footsteps stopped directly below the spare room. The front door opened with the same creak it had made when the girl let him in from the rain last night, soaked to the skin.

After a few shallow breaths, Michelle had recovered from her fright. Jim let go of her and felt the mattress tremble along with her body. Gradually she grew calmer and they lay still, next to one another.

'Sorry,' she said.

Jim laid his arm in the same spot, the hollow between her ribs and her hips. A beautiful slope, he thought. He said so, too. She gave a shy laugh. Her breathing grew faster as his hand slid down to touch the soft skin beyond.

With small movements of his finger he gradually pulled up her nightdress and felt the seam slide up his bare shin. The curtain rose, agonisingly slowly.

Michelle whispered that she had promised her dad she'd be very careful till she turned 18. Jim only half-listened. There was no need to be afraid, he said. He wouldn't hurt her. Did she really want to know what racing over the cobbles of Belgium could do to a man? Here, feel how battered and bruised he was. Yes, that bruise there, on his left hip.

The front door slammed shut. From the spare room, Jim heard someone shuffle down the hall. The squeak of a door was followed by the rattle of a drawer heavy with a full complement of cutlery. From pastry forks to serving spoons.

What's the difference between 17 and 18? That's what he had asked Michelle as he stroked her shoulder. The curtain had been raised. His hand left the nightdress bunched around her neck and glided down her body and over her breasts. She clamped her arms to form a barrier across her stomach and whispered another apology. Jim pressed a finger to her lips. Shhh.

Michelle lay there, her nightdress an innocent white ruff under her chin. With a few awkward tugs, he ripped open the press studs on the overalls and climbed on top of her. Her arms were still clamped tight against her stomach. She did not move them. Lost in the moment, Jim barely noticed.

. . .

THE LEGS OF A KITCHEN CHAIR SCRAPED LOUDLY ACROSS THE TILES. Jim now heard the shoes retrace their steps. The front door slammed again. He fastened up the press studs on the overalls, pulled on the boots and went downstairs.

Outside in the yard he saw a balding man in a raincoat. Michelle's father looked baffled at the sight of a young lad walking up to him dressed in one of his own overalls. Not sure what to expect, Jim held out his hand. 'Hello, I'm Jim.'

The man stuck out his own hand absently.

'Who are you? What are you doing here?'

'Jim, Jim Verhelst. I lost my way in last night's storm so I rang your doorbell and ...'

The man slapped him a little too hard on the shoulder.

'Well I never. Now I recognise you … Jim Verhelst! I don't believe it. The same Jim Verhelst who came third in Ourthe last month. Am I right? Yes, now I recognise you. You're a domestique with Shine Fine, aren't you?'

Jim stood in the middle of the farmyard, gobsmacked.

'That explains the racing bike by the fence. Come inside, lad. What are you still doing here? Aren't you racing the Tour des Ardennes? Ha, who'd have thought? A rider turning up here on my own farm. Where's Michelle?' The man looked at his watch and took two paces to the left so he could look past the barn.

Jim followed suit and saw a tractor off in the distance. Michelle was at the wheel, dressed in blue overalls identical to his.

Her father stuck two fingers in his mouth and whistled long and loud. Michelle turned and waved. 'She'll be a while yet. Come in, come in.'

A half-eaten cheese sandwich lay on a plate in the middle of the table. In the light of day, the kitchen looked completely different to the room where he had spent yesterday evening. The only familiar sight was the cheese beneath the tea towel over by the sink.

The cat jumped down from a chair and hissed long and deep, hackles raised, tail quivering.

'Mara!' Michelle's father charged towards the cat and almost landed a kick. As the animal fled outside, the farmer filled two cups with coffee from a Thermos can, took a scrapbook from a shelf and sat down at the kitchen table. Meanwhile the tractor rode back into the yard.

'Here, take a look at this.'

Jim turned the pages dutifully. One photograph after another showed Michelle's father standing beside famous cyclists. He recognised Felice Gimondi sporting some seriously warm headgear.

A smiling Frank Vandenbroucke, posing happily with his bike. Even Eddy Merckx, looking a little uncomfortable in his civvies, had taken the time for a snapshot. Michelle's father had documented each occasion: date, place and name of the race, written in a child-like hand.

Michelle came into the kitchen. She kissed her father on the lips, paid Jim no heed and walked over to the sink to wash her hands. The cat trailed along behind her, rubbing its head against her ankles.

'You're home early,' she said.

'Yeah, your Uncle Phil had to work today after all, so I thought I might as well head back.'

Michelle's father turned back to his photo album. 'Not a bad collection, eh?' he mumbled. 'And now you get to join 'em. You don't mind, do you? Michelle, be a love and fetch the camera.'

As she left the room, her eyes met Jim's for an instant. He saw fury.

Jim got to his feet. 'I'm sorry, mister, but it's gone ten. I really need to get a move on if I'm going to make the team bus in Malhay. The start's at 12.'

The farmer gulped down the rest of his coffee and nodded. He stood up and poked his head into the hall.

'Have you found it, Michelle? We need to hurry.' He turned to Jim, who was standing in the middle of the kitchen. 'Come on, let's take the picture outside.'

Jim sauntered over to his bike by the fence. Yesterday's mud had coated the frame grey.

The farmer grabbed Jim cheerily by the shoulder.

Michelle fumbled around with the old camera, as if she had never held it in her hands before. Her father barked instructions. She peered through the viewfinder and the two men waited for a flash that did not come. For seconds that seemed like minutes they held the same pose, her father with fixed smile, Jim aware of Michelle's gaze and unable to look straight into the lens.

'Yes! That button there!'

The flash came at last.

Michelle handed the camera to her father and marched back into the house without a word.

'Great. Tell you what, let me give you a lift to Malhay. It's a hell of a ride from here. You'll never make it by 12.'

Though the last thing he wanted was to listen to the farmer drone on endlessly about his encounters with the cycling greats, Jim knew it made sense. He accepted. As Michelle's father headed for the car, Jim detached his front wheel from the fork. His bike fitted snugly in the back seat.

• • •

'YOU HAVE A BEAUTIFUL DAUGHTER,' said Jim, as the car bounced over the narrow roads on its unyielding suspension.

'Yes,' said her father. 'The spitting image of my wife. Michelle's a beauty, all right. I'd invite you over when she turns 18,' he chuckled, 'but I don't think she goes in much for cyclists.'

They took the corners at speed and Jim was flung repeatedly against the door.

'They're a great bunch, cyclists. Never too busy for a photo with the likes of me. Salt of the earth, most of 'em. Even Zoetemelk. I met him during his final year on the circuit. Nice guy. Let me wear his cap for the photo.'

The farmer nattered on and Jim kept his eyes fixed on the road. Glancing down, he saw he was still wearing the blue overalls. Jesus! He could already hear the jibes from his teammates.

'Stop!'

Michelle's father slammed on the brakes. Jim shot out of his seat and his forehead slammed against the windscreen.

'What's up. Did I take a wrong turn?'

'We have to go back. I've forgotten my cycling gear.'

Michelle's father looked at the little clock on the dashboard. 'We're cutting it fine.' He turned the car at the first side road and raced back to the farm. 'The front door's open,' he shouted to Jim, keeping the engine running.

Jim rushed inside. The cat was there to greet him in the hall, hissing away as usual. It pounced as he hurried past and he felt sharp claws catch the leg of the overalls.

The bathroom was locked. On the other side of the door he could hear water gushing into the bath.

He knocked.

No answer.

'Michelle? It's me, Jim. Is my cycling gear still in there?'

The roar of the water grew louder. The taps had been turned on full.

'Michelle, can you hear me?' He pushed against the door but it wouldn't budge.

From outside came the frantic beeping of the car horn.

Jim pounded on the door. 'Michelle. Open up. Please. I'm in a hurry.'

Still no response. He battered his fist against the door.

Michelle's father had slammed his hand down and the horn blared long and loud.

Jim kicked the bathroom door. Then he clattered down the stairs, raced outside and jumped in the car.

'Couldn't find them?' Michelle's father asked.

'No,' Jim answered; his voice was tight, edgy. 'Please, let's just go. I'll never make it otherwise.' He fastened his seatbelt as the car spun around.

When they pulled out onto the road, it began to drizzle. Jim saw his own troubled face staring back at him in the mirror on the sun visor.

The car slowed ahead of a sharp bend. 'Don't worry, you'll make it,' the farmer shouted above the noise of the engine.

The rain turned heavy and the asphalt began to look slippery. Jim peered out through the fogged-up side window and wondered what caption Michelle's father would write under his photograph. Assuming it turned out all right.

FAUSTO NO MORE

Italy

FAUSTO LAY DEAD IN HIS COFFIN. Eyes closed, lips reduced to a thin crease. The life had drained from his lean face. Only his nostrils looked like they could still take in a deep draught of chill Piedmont air at any moment.

On 4 January 1960, 20,000 *tifosi* in their winter coats waited on the slopes around the village of Castellania. They had come to catch a glimpse of the coffin that held their departed *campionissimo*, their champion of champions. The sky was leaden. No hope of sun today.

How could the soul of Fausto Coppi have left his body at the tender age of 40? A body everyone thought was so strong?

Thanks to the intercession of Italy's minister of health, the dead rider's blood was examined by Professor Romanzi of the University of Genoa. The scientist discovered a parasite, *Plasmodium falciparum*. The presence of this minute creature pointed to the possible cause of death. Malaria.

Coppi was thought to have contracted the disease during his stay in Upper Volta, where he and French rider Raphaël Géminiani had planned to go crocodile hunting on the Pendjari River. But both men fell ill and made a hasty return to Europe, flying from Abidjan Airport on 18 December.

Until the final hours before his death, Coppi was treated as a patient suffering from a mysterious strain of influenza. News of the botched diagnosis was met with horror by his family and fury by his fans, especially when it emerged that Géminiani had returned home to France with exactly the same symptoms but had received the right treatment and survived.

The Italians felt they had been cheated of their greatest cycling hero. Coppi's body was placed on a bier at the supporters' club in his birthplace, Castellania. Hordes of people shuffled past his open coffin. He lay beneath a white sheet, the crucifix on his chest a reminder of the Catholic upbringing the pious claimed he had betrayed by running off with another woman.

A metal lid separated Coppi from the open air once and for all, a lid with a small pane of glass above his face. The bier was too high for Coppi's young son Angelo Fausto. Little Angelo's grandmother held him so that he could lean over and see through the tiny window.

Papa lay sleeping. Comfy on a bed of white satin. If Papa had been alive, the pane would have misted from the inside. But the glass remained clear and Papa stayed perfectly still.

Coppi Junior looked on as a group of burly men began to seal the coffin. Never again would a well-wisher pat the rider good-heartedly on his slender chest, home to an enlarged heart and lungs with a capacity of 6.7 litres. Never again would people gaze in admiration at the sober musculature of his legs, a little too long for his body.

During years of racing, the sole right to touch the *campionissimo*'s body had belonged to blind masseur Biagio Cavanna. Those who had seen him at work said the sightless man saw with his fingertips. Cavanna also saw to Coppi's inner workings. One week before the 1953 world championships in Lugano, he had given his rider a drink spiked with strychnine. On the day of the race, water bottle brimming with pure caffeine, Coppi had won the rainbow jersey. Cavanna stood beside the coffin, a broken man. He would never feel the warmth of Coppi's body again.

Coppi passed away on the second day of January in a hospital bed in Tortona. Time of death: quarter to nine. His wife Bruna Ciampolini and the later love of his life Giulia Locatelli, the White Lady, were close to their Fausto when he died. They remained close as he lay in state in the supporters' club, but did not stand next to each other if they could help it.

The final rituals by the coffin were too much for Giulia and she passed out briefly. The White Lady swooned in her black-lace headscarf, spasms of grief to which Coppi's stiff features could no longer respond.

Fellow riders were among those who carried the coffin through the streets of Castellania to the grave. They walked among slopes where the young Fausto had learned his craft, lugging rolls of salami and mortadella uphill and downhill on his bike as a 13-year-old errand boy for Merlani the butcher. His climbing muscles had developed from an early age.

Among the pallbearers was Gino Bartali. The Tuscan was Coppi's eternal rival and had ridden thousands of kilometres at Fausto's side. At his side, sometimes ahead of him, more often than not behind him.

It was a magnificent gesture that Bartali of all people should set his shoulder under Fausto's coffin. Bartali in his Sunday best, tie neatly knotted, long winter coat buttoned tight, hair slicked neatly back. He walked with dignity past the long rows of Coppi aficionados that lined both sides of the road.

At the cemetery in Castellania, a host of celebrated road masters stood ready to pay Coppi their last respects. Bobet, Anquetil, Kübler, Baldini, Binda. But it was Bartali who laid a wreath and made a sign of the cross. Bartali who, like Fausto, had lost a brother to cycling and whose steadfast faith told him they would see each other again one day.

In the months after Coppi's death, Castellania became a place of pilgrimage. French cycling enthusiasts arrived in the village bearing boxes of soil from the Galibier and the Col d'Izoard. Since Coppi was six feet under, it was only fitting that he should be surrounded by the ground he had covered on the tyres of his Bianchi. Ten years later the champion was disinterred. Fausto and his brother were given a new resting place, a grand tomb in the heart of Castellania.

Coppi's son is still with us. How often does Angelo think back to 4 January 1960, the day when he looked through a tiny window and saw his father for the last time? The boy had stared blankly at his father's face, a face framed in thousands of photographs while it was still full of life.

Pictures to last an eternity.

Coppi, brow beaded with sweat, reaching the top of a mountain pass.

Coppi, beaming with pride, playing with his son in the grass.

Coppi, burying his nose in the White Lady's black hair.

Pictures and memories. All we have since the day when a small pane of glass came between Fausto and the world.

MONTALTO

Italy

THE HILLSIDE WAS DOTTED WITH CYPRESSES; long green plumes that hid the spire of the village church from view.

I had studied the route back at the hotel. Tiny arrows were printed along the line on the map. One arrow meant the road was steep, two meant steeper still, and three meant the gradient could be as high as 20 per cent.

Taking a determined grip on my handlebars, I began the climb. The road rose steadily for the first kilometres and before long I hit a decent rhythm.

It was the churchyard, not the church, I was aiming for. A relative of Enzo Scorpio, my young Italian teacher in Rotterdam, lay buried there. Whenever Enzo heard that one of his students was holidaying not far from the north Italian village, he asked a small favour of them: to tend the grave of his uncle, Gianluca Tassato. A simple chore, he had assured me, 15 minutes at most. It comforted him to know that his uncle's grave was being looked after. Enzo hadn't been back for many years.

Approaching a hairpin bend, I spotted a dented metal sign at the side of the road, its blue faded by the sun. Without breaking my stride, I turned my head to see what it said. First came MONT, then came ALTO.

MONTALTO.

Enzo was a reserved young man who had arrived in Holland around ten years ago, aged 15. His parents had opened a delicatessen in the heart of Rotterdam, specialising in Italian wines and cheeses. Enzo attended the international school in The Hague and on graduating, he started teaching Italian at evening school. After two years of taking his classes, I still knew nothing about him. His friendly eyes never held your gaze for long. Enzo took a tentative approach to life.

The map had promised me a four-kilometre climb on a dead-end road. A succession of bends caused me to lose sight of the top.

Two arrows. A steeper section. I felt my calves tighten. I stayed up on my pedals till the going got a little easier. Passing the ruin of a farm building, I narrowly avoided a flattened hedgehog in the middle of the road. Some of its spines were still upright, the rest were broken needles scattered across the asphalt.

The final kilometre had two tough stretches in store. I had to stand out of the saddle again to maintain my pace. This was the steepest part of the climb. Three arrows for sure.

The asphalt gave way to a surface of large, flat stones. The road began to even out and the houses of Montalto came into view. A workman was perched on a ladder, plastering the wall of the first house. He saw me struggling up the hill and shouted something I couldn't understand. My attempt to smile back must have looked more like an anguished grimace.

To cool down after my exertions, I took a spin around the village square. A bar was tucked away in a corner with two tables and a cluster of chairs outside in the burning sun. Not a soul in sight.

I cycled to the end of the narrow road and arrived at the church. Having leaned my bike against the little building at the entrance to the churchyard, I pulled my bottle free of its holder and filled it with water running from a rusty tap.

It was a modest cemetery surrounded by a wall. Four parallel paths led past the graves; rows of sober headstones punctuated by the flourish of an occasional family tomb.

Tassato. That was the name I had to find. Enzo had given me exact directions, but I had forgotten to bring them with me.

I started down the first path to the left and automatically slowed my pace. The dead demand restraint. I thought back to my father's funeral on an ice-cold winter's day a few years earlier. The radio weatherman had warned that it would feel like –20°C, a chill factor to slice through countless layers of clothing. It was slippery underfoot and the undertaker was in two minds as to whether the family should be allowed to carry the coffin from the hearse to the grave. We shrugged off his objections. My father had been a frozen-food wholesaler. This was the temperature he worked in. No tribute more fitting. The undertaker conceded reluctantly. He and three of his colleagues walked alongside us with arms outstretched, as if a pile of dishes might crash to the ground at any minute. I swear our pace that day had worked its way into my muscle memory. Searching for balance with every step on the frozen gravel, shouldering my share of our dead father's weight.

Piano, piano.

The air in the churchyard was warm and sweet. Heavy with the smell of overripe fruit. Over the wall was an orchard, trees laden with apples. Two rows from me, a young woman crouched at a grave, arranging freshly picked flowers in a stone vase that was part of the headstone. A daisy chain hung around the neck of a marble angel. She looked up at the sound of my footsteps. A broad, beautiful face, dark deep-set eyes, flowing brown hair. I gave her a friendly nod and averted my eyes. I had no business interfering in the sorrow of a stranger.

Water bottle in hand, I continued to walk past the graves. Young and old lay side by side. Gianni Vernasco, a little boy of two, who had died in 1967. A plain concrete headstone, crumbling at the edges. Stefania di Luca, aged 101, shared her grave with Giorgio Dancelli, aged 93; Stefania had waited a long time to be reunited with her husband.

Tassato.

Found him!

It was the last grave on the left, before the wall brought the path to an abrupt end. GIANLUCA MARIA TASSATO, 4 FEBBRAIO 1937 – 16 SETTEMBRE 2002. An oval frame containing a black-and-white photo was attached to the headstone. Enzo's uncle appeared to be around 50, smiling for the camera. He was missing a tooth, his left incisor.

Ripe apples had dropped onto his gravestone and rotted. A bombardment of fruit that had attracted ants in their thousands, marching up and down in long disciplined lines. The insects emerged from the heart of the black-brown apples, filed past the engraved letters and disappeared into a hole in the dry earth.

'Well, Gianluca, time to give your sleeping quarters a good clean,' I murmured.

I put down my water bottle, picked up a fallen branch with leaves still attached and began to sweep the apples from the grave. The ants scattered in all directions. I rinsed the sticky patches from the grave with a few spurts from the water bottle.

'Those apples, *un disastro.*'

Her voice was deep for such a young woman. I had not heard her approaching. Her hands were dirty from the soil, brown streaked with green from the stems of her fresh flowers.

I pressed down the spout of my bottle and reckoned it must still be half full.

'The church keeps asking the man who owns the orchard to cut back the branches that hang over the wall, but he never does. Are you a cyclist?'

'No, just a tourist. From Holland.'

'Then why the ITALIA shirt?'

I shrugged sheepishly. 'Uh ... the country, the atmosphere, the language ... the ladies.'

There was a recurring hic in her laugh. Her front teeth were perfectly aligned.

She swung her leg and the toe of one of her white Nikes connected with a rotten apple. It hit a gravestone with a dry thud and a little cloud of mould flew up.

'I love these apples early in the season. I take them home for baking. Cover a hard base with slices of apple, one hour in the oven and they're soft and thick as jam. But at this time of year I hate them. There's no keeping this place clean.'

I looked around. Apples everywhere, scattered among the graves by the wall. I heard rustling and spotted a salamander darting off among the dry leaves by Tassato's headstone.

'You're Tassato's second visitor this summer. A couple came to tend to his grave two weeks ago. They were from Holland too. I didn't meet them myself but I heard about it in the village. Did Enzo send you?'

'Yes. Do you know him?' I asked.

The young woman rolled a pebble under the ball of her foot. 'Enzo. Yes. He used to live here in the village.'

I saw a flicker of hesitation in her face, as if she had something more to say. Instead, she changed the subject.

'What gear were you in on the climb to the village?'

'It was 21 or 23, I think.'

'Not bad.'

'Do you cycle yourself?'

'Of course. Everyone in the village has a bike. We start young. Everything worth having comes from the valley.'

An old woman passed along Tassato's row carrying a bucket of water to one of the grander tombs in the churchyard. Nose in the air and not so much as a glance in our direction.

'The widow of the former mayor,' the young woman whispered. 'He's buried here too.'

I stuck out the tip of my tongue. She giggled so loudly that she had to clasp her hand to her mouth. An infectious sound.

The widow set the bucket down next to a white marble tomb with a bust above the entrance. She lifted a sponge from the bucket and pressed it against the stony ridges of her husband's hair. Soap suds ran down his face.

I looked back at Enzo's uncle's grave. Tassato. The water on the gravestone had evaporated into the warm air. I took a swallow from my bottle.

'Who was Tassato?' I asked.

The young woman was silent for a moment.

'He was the village photographer. My parents took me and my sister to be photographed in his studio when we were little.'

She had found a new pebble to roll under the sole of her shoe. When it escaped, she shot it hard against the wall.

'I'd better get back to my flowers,' she said, and walked up the path.

'Okay, *ciao*,' I replied.

Another apple landed on Tassato's grave. A harder one this time. It rolled off the stone and landed at my feet. I picked it up, sprinkled it with water from my bottle and took a bite.

Sweet and sour.

Out of the corner of my eye, I could see the young woman kneeling by the grave further along. There were too many elaborate headstones between us for me to see what she was doing.

I settled down on a bench against the wall and gnawed away at the apple until I could taste the pips, then threw the core away. From where I was sitting I could just see my bike by the entrance. I felt reassured. No bicycle thieves in these parts.

Tassato's grave was looking presentable again. Enzo had asked for a photograph. I took my phone from the back pocket of my jersey and looked at the image of his uncle, within the confines of the little oval frame. A photo refuses to be photographed. I took my time with the camera settings and snapped two pictures – one vertical, one horizontal – and then strolled back to my bike.

From behind came the crunch of quick steps on the gravel. The young woman was hurrying to catch up with me. The low angle of the sun accentuated the sharpness of her profile. 'I have some business to attend to in the valley. If you don't mind waiting a moment, we can cycle down together.'

She walked across the square, her hips swaying gently, a lilt in every step. Her jeans stopped halfway down her calves, which had the same golden tan as her arms.

I felt a fluttering in my stomach. What had I done to deserve this? An invitation from a beautiful woman in an idyllic Italian churchyard, a woman who wanted to cycle down to the valley with me. Who would believe it? Enzo perhaps, but he was a stranger here now.

The woman swept out into the square on a faded orange bike with straight handlebars and mudguards front and rear. The brake cables ran along the frame, the good old-fashioned way. As we cycled to the corner of the square together, I stole a glance at the down tube. An old Gios. The girl had taste.

Once the flagstones of the square were behind us, the asphalt road remained even for another 50 metres before plunging towards the valley. We started our descent. I let her go first. She knew the way.

My Italian beauty rode without a helmet, her hair flowing freely in the breeze. She cornered tightly, fearlessly, pointing out irregularities in the road like a true *patron* of the peloton. Every extension of her finger revealed a loose stone or a dangerously wide crack in the road with precious seconds to spare.

'Does the downhill run scare you?' she shouted.

'I don't have the guts to go as fast as I used to.'

'No point being scared.' She slowed till I was cycling next to her. 'There's always a risk. And if you fall, then you fall. Remember number 108 in the 2011 Giro?'

'You mean Wouter Weylandt? The Belgian?' I yelled above the noise of the wind.

'*Si, si,*' she said, with a shake of the head. She made a little sign of the cross, kissed her fingertips and pointed skywards.

During a descent in the third stage of the Giro d'Italia, Weylandt had been travelling at high speed to catch the leading group. He looked to the side and lost his balance. His pedal scraped a low wall and he was dashed against the asphalt.

The images of Weylandt lying there motionless were still etched on my mind. Blood pouring from his head, dark red trails on the road's dull surface.

His girlfriend had been a few months' pregnant when he fell. Apparently no reason for the Belgian to ease up on the pedals or hold back as he took the bend. Every rider risks a fall; it's an integral part of life in the saddle. But they cannot acknowledge the spectre of death. Thinking of falling saps your speed.

My Italian beauty kept pedalling in the next bend and cut across the road like a time-trial specialist. She was a good ten metres in front of me. I recognised the ruined farmhouse I had passed on my way up.

We were halfway down. I trusted my guide implicitly. Her bike might be old but she seemed perfectly relaxed tucked low over the handlebars, betraying no doubts at all. We rounded the hairpin bend. From here it was only a few hundred metres to the main road through the valley.

At the T-junction, the young woman indicated left. My hotel was to the right, but she pointed emphatically to her back wheel, insisting that I stay on her trail.

We turned onto a wide road that ran parallel to the river. She slowed and rode beside me at an easy pace. The unbroken white line down the middle of the road was faded and skid marks scored the asphalt. The locals clearly had their own definition of road safety.

Old plane trees lined the road, close enough to touch. Each tree was daubed with a band of white paint at eye level, probably in an attempt to make them more visible to night drivers.

We were approaching another bend, a sharp one. She waved her hand, a signal for me to slow down. I squeezed my brakes and followed her around the bend.

'*Alt!*' she shouted.

She braked. So did I.

Once the bend was behind us, we pulled up on the right-hand side of the road and lay our bikes in the verge.

She ran her hand over the flaky bark of the nearest plane tree. It was only when I came and stood beside her that I saw what she was looking at. A small wooden shrine had been nailed to the tree, the size of a birdhouse but open at the front. The floor was strewn with little plastic roses and laminated prayer cards of the Virgin Mary. A photo was pinned to the back wall. A picture of a girl in a summer dress, a cap on her head and a big smile on her face. She looked around 16. Flawless skin, perfect teeth. Behind her was a strip of sea.

'Martina. My little sister.'

My Italian beauty looked longingly at the photo, as if she might be able to coax her sister to step out of it. Then she turned to the grass verge and picked a few stalks of clover. She smelled them and scattered them on the floor of the little shrine.

'Is this where she died?'

She walked away from me, stopped after a few metres, gauged the distance to the tree and traced a shape in the dust at the side of the road with her shoe: the outline of a body.

'Was she hit by a car?' I asked.

She stared at the ground and a lock of hair fell in front of her eyes. I couldn't bring myself to ask another question. I felt like an interrogator, a man so bent on extracting information that he won't give sorrow room to breathe.

She brushed the stray lock behind her ear and traced a circle beside the outline she had just drawn.

'Enzo.'

Next to that she traced another.

'Me.'

Without looking at me, she leaned out into the road and peered around the bend. She glanced the other way, then back at the bend.

A twinge of hesitation ran through her taut body. Then she sprinted across the road.

I heard the sound of a lorry's engine shifting down a gear. It rounded the bend with beer barrels rattling, less than a metre from the verge. My shins were peppered with loose stones.

Through the cloud of dust I saw her draw another circle with her shoe at the other side of the road. She pointed at it and shouted.

'Tassato!'

Since we had abandoned our bikes by the roadside, the suppleness seemed to have vanished from her body. Her movements seemed tense, more angular.

Again she looked anxiously from right to left, checking twice. Poised like an athlete at the start of a cross-country race, she took one more look and sprinted towards me.

Three cars towing caravans approached. Dutch number plates. They were still driving at a tidy pace as they took the bend. The tyre of the last caravan stirred the roadside chippings. The road was so narrow that even the traffic on the other lane felt oppressively close.

She was quiet for a while and brushed the same stray lock behind her ear.

'The three of us had cycled down from the village. Martina, Enzo and I. The annual regional cycle race was coming past. It was already busy when we arrived. Enzo decided we should stand here by the trees, so the sun wouldn't be in our eyes.'

She arranged the flowers in the little shrine as she spoke.

'Martina and Enzo were standing beside each other with their bikes between their legs. I was standing next to them. I remember a police motorcycle coming past, and then the leading group. You could feel the wind on your face as the riders flashed around the bend at top speed.'

She picked apart two prayer cards that had stuck together and blew on them three times. She ran her thumb over one of the cards and the sky above the Virgin Mary's devout face turned blue again.

'Before long the peloton came past. All those colours, those helmets, those flushed, tired faces.'

She placed the polished picture of Our Lady back in the shrine.

'Then came the stragglers, some in groups, some alone. Tassato was on the other side of the road, taking photos of the race for the local paper. Enzo shouted to his uncle to take a picture of the three of us. Tassato raised his thumb. And then ...'

She brushed the stray lock away again but it fell back in front of her eyes.

'Enzo pulled Martina closer. Since that spring he had been crazy about my little sister. You'd see them together every afternoon in the village. He pulled her closer and their handlebars locked. Martina lost her balance and took a step forwards.'

She bowed her head and her hair hid part of her face. She twirled a stalk of clover between finger and thumb till it grew soft. Then she walked back to the spot where she had traced the outline of the body. She sank to her knees and swept her arms forwards.

'My sister and her bike fell out into the road just as a car came around the bend. One of the last in the caravan.'

She walked over to the tree shrine with the determined air of a woman who has made a decision. She unpinned her sister's portrait and wriggled two fingers into the plastic sleeve that held the photo. Something was hidden away behind the smiling girl. Without a word, she pulled it out and handed it to me.

She crossed her arms and watched me unfold the yellowed paper.

It was a page torn from a newspaper, most of it taken up by a photo of a group of people at the side of a road, the sun behind them. In the middle a boy and a girl stood side by side, their bicycles leaning together. They were kissing awkwardly, probably because they were still trying to look at the camera. A boyish girl was standing next to them with a broad smile on her face.

The young woman was looking over my shoulder.

'I wore my hair short back then.'

She ran a finger across the paper. The white tip of her fingernail followed the road and stopped at the photo's edge. I saw the blur of a wheel. The bumper of a speeding car.

'That evening I went to Tassato's studio. I begged him to send this photo to the paper. It was my way of keeping my sister alive.'

Sure enough, the name under the photo read Gianluca Tassato.

'See how she's laughing, flirting?' she said.

'Did she die then and there?' I asked.

She ignored me and kept on talking. The story had to come out. She couldn't keep it in. It was like the urge to throw up. First nausea and disgust, then relief.

'Tassato rushed across the road and lay Martina on the verge. I held her head still. Blood was coming from her ears. Bystanders stopped the traffic. Tassato was down on his knees trying to resuscitate her. He called to Enzo to cycle to the doctor's, a kilometre down the road. I don't know how long Tassato fought for her life. The minutes ticked by. Fifteen maybe. Pumping at her chest, pressing his mouth to hers. When Enzo returned with the doctor, he must have seen instantly that it was too late.'

We stood and stared at the photo together. I didn't dare tell her, but it was a perfect composition. As if everyone in shot was aware that this scene had to be captured in one take. A split second of happiness before things changed forever.

I folded the page back up into a little square and handed it back to her.

'Does Enzo ever come here?' I asked.

'No, he moved to Holland a few months after the accident and we never saw him again. I can understand that. What's left for him here? He knows I tend to Martina's grave and this little shrine, he takes care of his uncle from a distance. Enzo and I keep our contact alive through the dead.'

She turned and walked away, slipped the newspaper cutting behind Martina's photo in the plastic sleeve and pinned it to the back of the shrine once again. She rearranged the flowers and the fresh clover. Then she brought her face close to the shrine and whispered.

I looked down politely. The white of her trainers had turned grey in the roadside dust. For the first time I noticed the long loops in her laces. Dangerous. They could easily get caught between her pedals.

Silently she rubbed out the lines she had traced in the dust, even dashing across the road to erase the circle that stood for Tassato. Again she looked three times before crossing.

She picked up her bike and I followed suit. We stood together at the side of the road.

'Where are you going?' she asked.

'Back to my hotel, in Bagni di Lucca. And you? Up to the village?'

She nodded. 'Yes, back to my husband and my baby.'

I took a swig from my water bottle.

'Want a drink?'

She reached for the bottle and missed. It fell to the ground and rolled into the road. Before we could move, a car came hurtling around the bend. It drove straight over the bottle, sending water spurting in our direction. My Italian beauty bent over laughing and wiped the drops from the legs of her jeans. She made another futile attempt to tuck that stray lock behind her ear.

'*Ciao,*' she said, and kissed me on the forehead.

'*Ci vediamo,*' I answered, hoping it was true. That we would see each other again.

'*Volentieri*. I'd like that.'

She swung her leg over the orange frame and perched on the edge of her saddle. Three times she looked left and right, once more for luck and she was off. A few strokes of her pedals and she had disappeared from view.

Alone again. Next to the plane tree I saw our footprints in the dust, all mixed together. Martina smiled down from her shrine. The little wooden shelter reminded me of a changing cabin at the beach. The swell of the sea at her back.

I mounted my bike, looked left, looked right then left again. That seemed like enough to me.

BARTALI'S ATTIC

Italy

GINO BARTALI'S PARCHMENT HAND GLIDES OVER THE OLD TYRES. The rubber has been worn to the thread, deflated tubs studded here and there with tiny stones. Stones from a famous race, a misty descent perhaps during a mountain stage of the Tour de France. Or grit from a Tuscan country road, inadvertent souvenirs picked up on one of his last training runs close to home.

The legendary Bartali is standing in the dim light of his attic, beside a row of bikes, their paintwork peeling. His hand takes hold of a frame with the casual assurance of a rider who knows precisely how high his seatpost should be. But no more hex keys for Gino. No worries about a saddle-sore backside. No need to check the links on the chain. For Gino that's all in the past.

Yet in this room full of testaments to Bartali's glory days, a hint of fanaticism creeps back into the elderly body of Italy's most down-to-earth rider, the people's champion.

One floor down his wife Adriana is shuffling invisibly through the rooms. Her wrinkles fail to dampen her girlish smile. She must have been a beauty in her day. The lipstick she's wearing is a touch too pink and leaves its imprint on her coffee cup. She is the pilot light of Gino's existence, watching over his diary, his appointments, his nap times. Gino is well into his eighties and has already had a few perilously close encounters with the sweet hereafter.

On the phone he had sounded congested. An interview? Yes, drop by tomorrow morning after 11. In Ponte a Ema, just outside Florence. No more than half an hour, Adriana had shouted in the background. Gino wasn't in the best of shape, recovering from a *broncopolmonite*. Pneumonia.

Now, walking back and forth beneath the slanting attic beams, his eyes light upon every trophy, every laurel wreath, every certificate and racing bike with the look of love a grandfather usually reserves for his grandchildren.

'I have no need to leave this place again. This is the land of my birth. Close to Florence, the most beautiful city in the world. Tuscany. Tafi, Cipollini, both strong men. They too are Tuscans. Here is where my memories lie.' Bartali walks over to an old frame. 'Look, this was the bike I won Milan–San Remo on, in 1950. At least I think it is.'

He leans forwards and fiddles with a steel cable. 'See how simple our brakes were then,' he says, scraping a layer of dirt from behind a brake pad. *'C'è un po' di gomma.'*

I savour every word of Italian that comes from the old man's lips. *Un po' di gomma*. A little piece of rubber. Marlon Brando's Godfather pales in comparison with the rasp of Bartali. Brando? Who needs him? A self-obsessed softy too lazy to do a hard day's work. Cheeks stuffed with sopping wads of cotton wool.

My allotted half-hour was up long ago. The sly old fox knows damn well that his wife is downstairs keeping an exasperated eye on the clock. But for now the race is on. Bartali was never one to give up, not even here in his attic. In his day, women had no place in cycling. They were left by the roadside or stood waiting at the finish. Here, in the belly of his own museum, he is bringing those days back to life. Bikes, friends, foes, klaxons, back-up cars, *tifosi*, dirt tracks, empty water bottles, spare tyres slung around the shoulders.

He points at the engraving on a large silver trophy. '*Coppa della Montagna* in the Giro of 1936. That's what it says, isn't it?'

I can't make out the words and ask where the light switch is.

'*No, non c'è luce.*' There is no light.

He would love to see his prizes in a museum. He knows it's an honour he has earned, that his victories deserve a place in the light again.

'The local council talks about it, so does the cycling association … but you know how it is in Italy: all talk and no action. *Troppo politica*. Too much politics. It's a shame. Just look at all these trophies. Prizes and more prizes, enough to make your head spin. Here, another *premio della Montagna*. A mountain win from … 1947 … 1948? I was supposed to return the trophy to the association. But what has the association ever done for me? *Nulla*. Nothing. So I kept it myself. I want to see all these things in a museum before I die, close to home if possible. For as long as I live, I'll give nothing away. To no one.'

In the gloom behind the muddle of prizes, I count stacks of cardboard boxes, packed with yet more memories of Bartali's career. Stuff the *tifosi* would kill to get their hands on. Every object associated with Bartali is a thing of value and Bartali knows it. Each year he puts in an appearance as a mascot at the Giro or Milan–San Remo. With a cycling cap from the publicity caravan slapped on his bald head, he waves at the crowds and twice as much at the cameras. Addicted to the spotlight, to anything that smacks of cycling. The people adore him. In his twilight years he's become a showroom dummy for Italy's grand cycling tradition, a Michelin man come to life. It saddens me to see him in his cheapo headgear plugging some random product, looking almost as pathetic as Frenchman 'Poupou' Poulidor, another veteran who never seems to get enough of waving from the Tour caravan.

Poupou et Gino. As a title for a cycling comic strip, it's hard to beat.

Bartali's fingers glide on, take hold of another frame. His voice gives a husky crack.

'*Piombino.*'

The little lead token.

Gino fingers a small black disc hanging from the handlebars.

'If you crossed the border on your bike, you had to get one of these from customs. This one here is to pass from France into Belgium. You always had to pay the toll yourself and get your money back at the border on your return leg.'

In his blue polo shirt, he stares at a clapped-out exercise bike in among the other bikes. It looks like a relic from the 1970s. No sign of a digital display on the handlebars. The frame is square and bulky.

'Can't cycle outdoors any more. I'm just not up to it. But up here in the attic, I can still manage on that thing. Easy does it, though. *Piano, piano.* And only if I'm feeling right – 15 or 20 minutes without breaking into a sweat.'

Bartali at home on an exercise bike. Twenty minutes max. Steady on the pedals. Soldiering on at a decent pace. He knows you only pay for it at the end of the race.

'*Sono un diesel.*'

A diesel. A beast of an engine that keeps on rolling, three times around the clock. Never letting up. In the course of his career, he put in 150,739 kilometres on the road, almost 30,000 more than Coppi. In that respect he beat the rival he battled against on 416 occasions. A distance of 150,739 kilometres ... How many times around the world would that be?

Every now and then a cough and a sigh emanate from Bartali's body. He is 83. His heart is weak. He lets me feel the pacemaker he's had fitted. It's as if a draughts piece has found its way under his skin. 'I had no choice. At one point my heart rate was down to 37.'

* * *

ALMOST THREE YEARS LATER, I'm in Turin – 6 May 2000. At a bar on the Via Pietro Micca I order an espresso and pick up the sports paper. Headline news: Bartali is dead. At around two o'clock the previous afternoon he drew his last breath, aged 85. Top right, there's a photo in sepia tones: Bartali battling up a mountainside, solo. As he climbs, he swings his bike a little to the left, his front wheel following the unbroken line on the road. Supporters watch him go.

Addio Ginettaccio is the tender headline in the *Corriere dello Sport*. The paper reflects on how special an ordinary man can be. After ten pages in honour of Italy's cycling hero, I glug back my tepid espresso and walk to Piazza Solferino.

Bartali dead. On 5 May.

I try to remember his handshake when he met me at the door in Ponte a Ema. The smell of an ordinary Italian house on a square, the floor tiles in the living room, the narrow staircase up to the attic. 'Let me go first,' he said that morning, and ascended step by careful step. All the way up I was left staring at his backside. Buttocks that had withstood over 150,000 kilometres on a hard saddle.

Bartali dying in Florence. It's as if Cruyff had died in Amsterdam. At every sports venue in Italy, a minute's silence is held, 60 seconds to meditate on the man who was Bartali.

His wife Adriana had been there at his bedside in his final hours, together with their three sons. Gino had been hooked up to a drip, his heart weaker than ever. Out of the blue he began to talk about mountains. 'Which mountains do you mean?' one of them asked.

'All mountains,' he answered. 'There is not one I did not know.'

From then on, his breathing became weaker and weaker. After 85 years, his body had nothing left to give. For the first time in his life, Bartali knew what it was to be too tired to go on. Receiving the last sacrament a few days later, he was unable to swallow. The devout Catholic missed out on his final Communion wafer.

Adriana held him during his final minutes. Gino said nothing else. His eyes remained closed and his head slumped to the side. There was no sigh, no moan. They massaged his heart but in vain.

Suddenly it dawns on me that in the days leading up to Bartali's death, I've been walking around in the homeland of his great rival. Turin is the heart of Piedmont. And Piedmont means Coppi. Bartali talked about his rival that day in his attic, and the words come drifting back.

'Coppi ... Oh, Fausto is in heaven. With his brother Serse. They are happy together, as spirits. They have wings. They are birds, of a kind. Up in heaven there are no streets. No cars, no bikes, no traffic lights.'

The love with which Bartali spoke of Coppi that morning has always stayed with me. There is no need to sneer at a worthy opponent.

Bartali too had someone waiting for him in heaven: his little brother Giulio, another keen cyclist. He came to grief during a race in 1936, when a daring breakaway ended in tragedy. If Bartali is to be believed, he and Giulio, Fausto and Serse are four little birds now, flitting around up there. It's a comforting thought.

I can still hear the two words that rolled from Bartali's smiling lips that morning as he contemplated the final leg of his life. Confidently, he pointed skywards. There was only one direction possible.

'Andiamo su.'

Upwards we go.

BEND

Italy

I T WAS LIKE LOOKING at the world through a plastic bag. The trees were green smudges, the sky a vast smear of grey.

I felt a teardrop trickle across my temple. My eyes would not stop watering. I blinked and clocked the reading on the speedometer: 69kmph. In a flash my focus returned to the blur of asphalt ahead.

There's nothing quite like a descent: cycling reduced to raw guts, the guts to embrace speed. My weight bore down on my wrists. Squeezing the brakes would be sacrilege. Downhill experts slow before they hit the bend by catching just enough wind with their upper body. As they corner, they get aero and pile on the speed again.

The art of descent is all about the balance between faster and slower, pedals and brakes, brains and balls. Velocity can show you who's boss at any moment. And that's something you can never allow to happen.

That afternoon, I had set out from my hotel in Spoleto with the urge to wing it. This part of Umbria was hilly and rugged. The smooth roads on the first hour of my journey had sent me weaving through neighbouring villages. No chance to simply put my head down and go. I was constantly chopping and changing to avoid parked cars, roadworks, market stalls and dogs off the leash.

But after a while the landscape had gradually emptied out. The roads shed their markings and the traffic thinned to sporadic at most.

I blinked again to take another look at my speed: 71kmph. I tucked in lower, till the tip of my nose was almost touching the handlebars. The bends here were ideal; I could line up the corners and still see enough to dodge an oncoming car.

A sign on the inside of the road announced another left-hand bend. I was feeling sure of myself. The asphalt surface was dry, I could easily take the bend just by hanging off to the side.

A seasoned cycling pro once told me the secret of the perfect bend. 'Never look too close in front of you' was his motto. He reckoned you could pick out irregularities in the road far better from a distance. If you only noticed a hole when it was metres from your front wheel, you had missed a trick. You should have seen it coming much sooner.

Here came my perfect bend. I swung my left knee out to the side. That's the way to do it. Get low without losing speed. Hands on the drops and lean to the side. Hip swung low. No sudden moves on the saddle. Left pedal raised clear of the road surface.

This was going well.

Okay, so the bend was a little tighter than expected.

But no need to panic.

My brain began buzzing. Leave those brakes alone! I saw the road sign: rusty pole, grass around it, longer than the rest of the verge. I saw a reflector strip, white plastic post, three crosshead screws securing strip to post.

Shit! I was going too fast.

I straightened up to catch more wind, slid hesitantly to the back of the saddle and tried to aim for the inside of the curve. In vain: I was drifting wider. No worries, none whatsoever. Just don't try any crazy manoeuvres. You've got all the time in the world to set things right.

I saw the jagged cracks in the asphalt below me, stones of different colours on the inside verge. My speed was forcing me to the outer edge. I looked up: no oncoming traffic. I was in luck.

Halfway around the bend. Despite staying upright, my speed was still too high. Braking would not be smart, every chance the wheel would slip out from under me. One metre of asphalt remaining to my right. I had to get myself back into the middle of the road. Should I brake after all?

I saw gravel on the road dead ahead. A scattering of small, loose stones.

Brake?

No.

Yes?

I braked and tugged on the handlebars.

Too late.

IT WAS QUIET. Conspicuously quiet. No more wind rushing in my ears. I turned my head and looked around. I was lying off to the side of the road, spreadeagled on a bed of prickly branches. Road on one side, valley below me on the other.

Pain shot through my left shoulder, like the twisting of a blade. Tentatively, I pulled my arm towards me and felt thorns dragging across my skin.

I was lying on my back in the bushes, staring up at the sky. Slowly I brought my chin to my chest. Red lines scored my arms and legs. I was unable to lift my left arm any higher. Thankfully my right seemed to be in working order.

I touched my cheek and looked at my fingertips. Blood.

I tried to reach down and touch the ground. Not even close. Branches and thorns everywhere. Another jolt of pain to my left shoulder.

Was my collarbone broken? How many cyclists had I seen clutching their clavicle as soon as they hit the deck?

The momentum had flung me a good three metres from the road. I turned my head the other way and saw that the hillside beneath me dropped away steeply into the valley. Not a great place to land. I needed help. There was no way I could extricate myself from these bushes alone.

I swallowed hard and tried to focus. How many thorny branches surrounded me. Fifty? Sixty? I tried to pull one loose, but it was so strong and stubborn that it shot straight back into position. I tried another, but it was just as determined not to budge.

In the distance I heard a car approaching. Judging by the sound of the engine, it was shifting up a gear. Would the driver be able to spot me? There were an awful lot of branches in the way.

The drone grew louder. I waved my good arm and began to scream. 'Help, help!'

Through the bushes I saw the shape of a car. Red. An Italian number plate.

'Aiuto!' I yelled in schoolbook-Italian.

My voice was drowned out and, as it roared around the bend, I saw the car was actually a van. AC Milan bumper sticker. A northerner in a hurry.

It was late afternoon and the sun was obscured by a grey blanket of cloud. I could feel the blood pounding in my shoulder, as if it was thumping to gain access to the joint.

My eyes came to rest on my bike, suspended on the bush next to me, undamaged by the look of it. I noticed that one of my cleats was still attached to the pedal. It must have been ripped off during the fall.

The realisation dawned that I was going to have to save myself. This was a sparsely populated region. The chances of another car rolling around the bend any time soon were slim. Like an idiot, I had left my phone back at the hotel. Why weigh myself down on a quick jaunt through the hills? Now I knew the answer.

The blue of my cycling shirt was a mess of stains, two shades of red. The bright red of blood from my cuts and a deeper red, verging on purple. For the first time I spotted the berries among the thorns. Brambles. I picked one and popped it in my mouth. Juicy, sweet. At least I could rule out imminent starvation as a probable cause of death.

The wind began to pick up and the darkening clouds threatened rain. I felt goose pimples rising on my sweaty skin. Surely someone would come wandering past? A nature-lover on a ramble in search of peace and quiet? Or were tourists a rarity in these parts?

An unwelcome memory swam into focus. A magazine article about a couple of holidaymakers, stranded in the Australian outback in a rented car. Pinpricks of humanity in a vast and hostile environment. Helicopter-borne rescue teams needed the eyes of a hawk to home in on lost souls out there in the wilderness. The couple had not been found in time.

My mind began to race. If someone did come along, I would need some way to catch their attention. I could wave my shirt in the air. But how was I going to take it off when I could barely move on my bed of brambles and the slightest movement of my left arm had me crying out in pain?

Would the hotel raise the alarm if I failed to return that evening? Perhaps they preferred to turn a discreet blind eye to the comings and goings of their guests or simply didn't give a toss. After all, they had nothing to lose financially. I pay for my pleasures well in advance, like a good little Dutchman.

In the distance I could hear another car approaching. Travelling uphill this time. The driver had a sporting way with his vehicle, changing gear frequently and double-clutching. The high-revving engine sounded positively hot-tempered.

I began screaming well before I saw anything, determined to seize this chance. Perhaps shorter bursts would be easier to hear.

'Hey-hey-hey-hey-hey-hey!'

The car came charging around the bend. It was clear my cry for help had not been heard. The engine's drone echoed off the flanks of the surrounding hills and ebbed away.

Again I tried to bend a thick branch away from my body. No chance. It thwacked back at me, stiff as a cane.

There I lay. A carcass served up on a bed of thorns. Flick on a lighter and I'd go up like Joan of Arc. I turned my head again and looked over at my trusty bike. Perhaps I could reach the bottle holder with my fingertips. Yes, I was just able to tap the bottom with my middle finger. I stretched as far as I could. One more push and the bottle would come loose. I wrestled a twig from the bush and, with a single thrust, managed to poke the bottle out of its holder. It dropped onto the thorny branches and rolled my way.

My luck hadn't run out just yet.

Isotonic sports drink had never tasted so sweet. I knew this bottle could save my life.

I had only one chance. If I could pitch the bottle clear of the bush, the driver of the next car – Christ, let there *be* a next car! – might see it flying through the air. Fingers crossed that would be enough to make them slam on the brakes.

I took one last swallow, careful not to drink too much. I needed weight in the bottle if I was going to control its trajectory.

At least half an hour had gone by since the last car. The grey afternoon was fading into dusk. I had begun to shiver constantly and the blood continued to pound in my shoulder. The bottle lay in my palm like a hand grenade.

Was it wishful thinking or were my ears picking up the distant whine of an engine off among the hills? Every now and then it faded, only to return just a little bit louder.

One last chance. Only one.

Timing was everything. A single swing of the arm, better too soon than too late, in the hope of punting the bottle into the driver's field of vision. Miss and I would be facing a night among the brambles.

The noise was clear now, higher pitched. I reckoned the driver must be braking as he came down the incline. Not a big car by the sound of it.

I closed my eyes and tried to focus on what I was hearing. By my estimate, the car must be around 100 metres away. I checked that the top of the bottle was shut and tossed it in my hand a few times to get used to its weight.

The sound increased in volume. I had to throw before the car came into view. Another few seconds.

The glow of headlights through the branches.

Now.

I stretched my arm, took a deep breath, lobbed the bottle over the bush and watched it fly. High enough? Quick enough?

The car rounded the bend and I stared into a thin beam of light. Where was the second headlight? Broken?

No. It was a motorbike.

The bottle hit the ground just metres from the front wheel. The top shot loose and the remaining liquid spattered into the air. Through the branches, I saw the rider swerve and brake. His tyres slipped. It was all he could do not to fall. He skidded to a halt at the very edge of the road.

I screamed for all I was worth.

'*Aiuto! Sono qui, aiuto!*'

I waved my good arm in the hope that my hand would peek out above the bushes. The rider stamped his feet down next to his bike. He couldn't have been more than a few metres away.

'*Qui, qui!*' I shouted excitedly.

The biker dismounted, pushed his bike to the side of the road and kicked his stand into place. He lifted the visor on his helmet. '*Stronzo. Faccia di cazzo!*'

His rage was palpable. He looked for a way to get to me, yelling all the while in Italian. From what I could make out, he either wanted to kill me or he was telling me I'd nearly killed him.

'*Scusi,*' I said, with a helpless, agonising shrug.

The biker was standing next to the bushes. I raised my head as high as I could. His eyes were blazing and I caught sight of a thick moustache above fleshy lips. The face of a man who was not to be messed with.

The headlight of his motorbike lit up the bushes. I pointed at my collarbone and grimaced, giving him my best imitation of bone snapping. 'Crrrkkkk!'

'Broke?' the rider asked.

I nodded.

He took a good look at the position of my body.

'One moment,' he said.

He walked back to his bike and hung his helmet on the handlebars. From under the saddle he produced a leather pouch. I heard the clanking of tools.

He turned and came towards me with a pair of wire cutters in his hand. Determinedly he grasped the base of a bramble branch and cut it loose.

'Grazie,' I said.

I lay there motionless as one by one the biker clipped away the branches around my head.

'Grazie mille.'

He kept on clipping, wiping the sweat from his forehead every now and again. He pulled down the zip of his jacket a little to reveal a red T-shirt with a low neck. As he cut, a little crucifix danced on a chain around his neck.

He began to clip away the branches around my upper body and gradually I was able to move. I helped him with my right arm, holding the branches steady as he cut and throwing them out of the way.

I tried to peel away one last thick branch that was resting on my legs. The biker took hold of it for me. One more clip and I would be able to move. Heaving a sigh of relief, I struggled loose and felt the thorns carve a few fresh wounds into my calf muscles.

Free at last.

The biker squatted beside me and took a closer look at my lacerated legs.

'No good.'

I clicked my helmet loose and laid it down beside me. Running my fingertips over my cheek, I felt a deep, sticky cut.

The biker reached into his jacket pocket, handed me a red kerchief and pointed at his cheek. I folded it in half twice and pressed it against the wound.

As I was dabbing at my cheek, a cheery ringtone burst from his jacket pocket. The sunny Italian melody triggered memories of long days at the beach. He pulled out his phone and pressed a key. He listened more than he spoke, an occasional *'si'* followed by a short, hurried question. His face stiffened and he looked at his watch.

'*Okay, vengo subito.*'

He hung up.

'What's the matter?' I asked.

He frowned and for a moment he said nothing.

'Hospital. My wife. Emergency. I have to go.'

He wiped the first raindrops from the display with his thumb.

'She is pregnant. The baby is coming. Too early.'

'How early?' I asked.

'Way too early. Twenty-seven weeks only. She's in hospital in Spoleto. I have to go. Now.'

I understood the urgency. But standing here in the dark, in the middle of nowhere, I couldn't exactly ignore my own predicament. His wife would be in good hands. Her heartbeat was being monitored, cold stethoscopes were gliding over her belly. A full drip was hanging ready on its hook.

'Can I come with you to the hospital?'

'What? On my bike? No. Sorry.'

The biker zipped up his jacket. He looked at his watch again and shook his head.

'Why not?' I asked.

'Because … Impossible,' he snapped back.

'But you can't just leave me here.'

'My bike is too small for two.'

I looked at his motorcycle. He had a point. There wasn't exactly much room on the saddle.

How could I convince him? I tapped my collarbone and left him in no doubt as to how much it hurt.

'You'll get your reward,' I said.

'How do you mean?'

The biker looked at me, baffled.

'I saw your crucifix. You know God will reward you.'

His eyes darted back and forth. He checked his watch again, immediately followed by his phone, and mumbled something I could not understand.

'Okay. We go. And pray to God we make it,' he said.

I handed him back his kerchief and he tossed it resolutely into the bushes.

I tried to block out the pain as I walked over to the motorbike, clamping my left arm to my stomach. My reluctant saviour donned his helmet and rocked his bike off its stand. He swung his leg over the saddle and gestured to me. I grabbed his shoulder with my good hand, eased myself into position and placed my feet on the rests. The saddle dipped towards the front and I slid into the back of him. My painful arm was trapped between my chest and his back.

'Okay?'

I gave him a thumbs up.

He lowered his visor and revved up the engine.

'Wrap your arm around my middle,' he yelled.

Feeling more than a little awkward, I slid my hand around his belly.

Cautiously he accelerated and we slowly pulled away. Away from the scene of my ordeal and away from my bike. At least it was hidden from view. With any luck it would still be there in the morning and I would be able to persuade the hotel to send a van to pick it up.

'How many kilometres?' I asked.

'Quattordici.' I hoped that meant 14 and not 40. 'Pain?'

'A little,' I said as I felt the blade twist in my shoulder again.

We could barely hear each other over the roar of the engine. The logo on the tank told me she was a good old make. Moto Guzzi.

The biker moved his body from side to side.

'You the same,' he shouted.

I understood: lean into the corners. I had to move my body with his.

The asphalt shone in the rain. Coming up to the first bend, I dug my nails anxiously into the biker's jacket and closed my eyes. We leaned to the left and the motorbike tilted into the bend. Exactly the same sensation as on the bike. I pressed myself firmly against him, to hell with the pain.

The biker cornered at high speed. I opened my eyes a fraction and saw his knee skimming mere centimetres above the road surface. Any sudden move on my part and we would come crashing to a halt. I closed my eyes again and surrendered to his helmsmanship.

The bend was followed by another. And another.

When I began to feel we were tilting less, I plucked up the courage to open my eyes. We straightened up after yet another bend, still in one piece. Ahead of us lay a long stretch of road that led straight into the valley.

The biker looked over his shoulder and raised his visor. I looked into his smiling face. Now we were on our way, his worries about his wife and baby seemed to be less of a burden.

'You forgot your helmet,' he shouted.

I pictured it lying at the roadside.

'Stupido!' I exclaimed.

The biker tapped his visor shut, looked straight ahead again and slid back in the saddle. He was probably used to sitting further from the handlebars.

I slid backwards too and felt another stab in my shoulder. I stifled a scream and the biker stepped on the accelerator. I peered over his shoulder: 110kmph on a narrow road, in the rain. His idea of safety wasn't mine.

In an attempt to show my gratitude, I tried to make contact with him again.

'The baby is your first child?' I asked.

'Yes, *primo*,' he answered, looking to the side.

We hit a slight bend. He barely slowed.

'*Vacanze?*' he yelled.

'Yes, yes.'

'*Solo?*'

'*Solo*, with the bike, yes.'

We passed a sign for Spoleto. Only four kilometres to go.

It seemed to spur the biker on to greater speeds. He slid further back in the saddle. I followed suit till I realised I was in danger of sliding off the back.

As the speedometer hit 120kmph, the biker looked around, bit the tip of his tongue and grinned. I had to cling on for dear life or risk being jettisoned.

Mercifully, he had to slow for a set of traffic lights. Civilisation was at hand. I saw the town ahead, nestled against the hillside. The biker raised a thumb and shot me a questioning look through his visor.

I nodded.

'Nervous?' I asked.

'My wife is strong.'

'What's her name?'

'Raffaella.'

The lights changed to green. I threw my arm back around his waist. We tore through the streets of Spoleto. Down a side street I glimpsed the sign above the entrance to my hotel. I yearned to pop a couple of painkillers and lower myself into a nice warm bath.

The roar of the motorbike echoed through the narrow streets. I caught sight of our reflection in a shop window: a middle-aged man in Lycra shorts clinging to the back of a leather-clad biker.

The road beneath us turned bumpier. Asphalt had given way to cobbles. I tested my collarbone by trying to move it gently. Was it fractured? Severely bruised?

A hospital building loomed up ahead. The biker slowed to walking pace and stopped in front of the entrance. He held out his arm to support me as I got off, then leaned his bike on its stand. He lifted the helmet from his head and tucked it under his arm. We walked into the building side by side, under the watchful eye of two patients smoking at the doorway, drips on wheels at their side.

The biker's smile had vanished. His thumb circled anxiously over the display of his mobile phone. He marched up to reception and hurriedly informed them why we were there. As he rattled on, he glanced my way every now and again.

'Take a seat around the corner to your left,' the receptionist said to me in calm Italian. 'We will help you as soon as we can.'

'*Grazie*,' was all I could reply.

The biker ran off in the direction of the maternity ward.

'All the best to you and your wife,' I shouted down the corridor. 'And to the little one.'

I saw the seam of his jeans sticking out from under the legs of his biker gear. Stonewashed.

I sat down on a plastic chair, next to a woman with a dishcloth wrapped around her thumb. The blood was seeping through. She studied my cuts and scratches with a frown.

'*Bicicletta*,' I said.

She nodded at her provisionally bandaged thumb and made a slicing motion with her other hand.

'*Pancetta*.'

A nurse came to fetch me and ushered me into a cubicle. While she attended to my cuts one by one, a doctor assessed the damage imperiously. He peered at me through off-kilter specs and tapped my shoulder and clavicle with his fingers.

'No broke,' he said, and made a swift exit.

The nurse fetched some pieces of gauze and cleaned my wounds with iodine. As she eased my arm into a sling, I thought of my bike lying in the bushes all those kilometres away. Abandoned. We would sleep apart tonight, my bike and I.

The nurse sat down at a little desk and filled in a sheaf of forms. Once I had recited my personal details, she placed a cross where I had to sign. Like many a left-hander, I was able to give it a decent shot with my right.

'No more *bici* this week,' she said with a schoolmarmish expression.

I blinked in a show of friendly obedience and stepped back into the hallway.

The clock told me I had been here for an hour already.

I found my way back to reception and asked for the maternity ward.

'Primo piano,' said the woman who had helped me earlier.

I took the lift to the first floor and found myself at another desk. A nurse looked up from her computer screen. Over her shoulder, I spotted a few men waiting in a corridor but the biker wasn't one of them. She asked me what I wanted. I cast around for the right words but this was pushing my Italian to the limit.

'Is there a driver in your department?'

She looked perplexed. As well she might.

'Uomo moto. Moglie ...' I traced the outline of a massive bump with my free hand.

'His name?'

I realised that I only knew the name of his wife. *'Sua moglie Raffaella.'*

She tapped away at the keyboard with two fingers and looked at her screen.

'Raffaella Cellini. Raffaella Vanoni. Raffaella di Napolitano.'

She looked at me enquiringly. Just my luck. Enough Raffaellas to start a girl group.

Through the glass wall of the maternity ward, I could see doctors, nurses and a couple of heavily pregnant women accompanied by their husbands.

'Raffaella 27 weeks,' I said, tracing another imaginary bump.

'*O dio ...*' Briefly she bit her lower lip.

'Dangerous?' I asked.

She nodded, more for her own benefit than mine. She pointed at me.

'Family?'

'No, friend.'

'*Passaporto? ID?*'

I shook my head and a mental image of the side pocket of my suitcase where I had tucked away my important documents floated into view.

'*Passaporto* in hotel,' I said.

The nurse pulled a sad face. 'Closed,' she said. Did she mean that this was a secure ward?

In another glass-fronted room at the end of the hall, I saw a couple of incubators. The nurse was right not to let me in. Cut to ribbons with my arm in a sling, I wasn't exactly the picture of health. And could I honestly say I was more concerned than curious? I stepped aside to make way for the man who was next in line.

When I took another look through the glass, I recognised the figure of the biker standing by one of the incubators. He was wearing what looked like a blue shower cap. A mask covered his nose and mouth. He ran his hands over his cheeks.

I raised a hesitant hand, thinking he might recognise my cycling jersey.

Yes, he raised his hand in reply.

Our eyes met for a moment.

I gave him a thumbs up.

He shook his head.

The glass distorted the image.

I had to narrow my eyes to see that his thumb was pointing down.

ADDIO, MARCO

Italy

WITH THE END IN SIGHT, one of the men shouldering Marco Pantani's coffin gives a sign. He can't go on. Someone will have to take his place. Via Mazzini, the street that leads from the church to the cemetery of Cesenatico, is long today. Both sides of the two-kilometre stretch are crammed with thousands of Italians, there to spur on their cycling hero one last time. He comes past at a snail's pace.

'Vai in paradiso! Grazie, Marco!'

A pair of fresh shoulders have been set under the coffin and amid loud applause it passes through the brick archway that leads to the cemetery. Fans run alongside, left and right. No one knows exactly where Pantani will be laid to rest.

At the cemetery, very little appears to have been organised. A group of Pantani supporters wearing yellow armbands set themselves up as stewards and try to clear a path for the family. The throng is hard to control. As soon as they see the coffin turn down another row, the onlookers try to cut the procession off at the pass in the hope of beating it to Pantani's final resting place.

The coffin comes to a halt in front of a long wall sheltered by a sloping roof, beneath a sign that says SECTION G, 201–400. There are gaps in the wall into which coffins can be slotted. A depot for the dead. No free-standing grand tomb for Pantani. Place 262 is empty; 262 will be his final race number. The sobering end of a cycling legend. A slot at a height of three metres, directly above Sotero Pantani, his grandfather, who passed away in 1992.

Fans appear from every nook and cranny to catch a final glimpse of the coffin. A couple of cameramen climb up a mobile ladder that cemetery staff use to lift the coffin to the right height. The press claiming this exclusive vantage point for themselves is a step too far for the self-appointed stewards.

'Bastardi, bastardi, bastardi!'

Amid shouts and screams, a cameraman is dragged down from the top rung and forced to hand over his footage. The tape disappears into the pocket of one of the stewards. More and more Italians have come to see the relentless press coverage of Pantani's downfall as the cause of his death.

Any intimate moment for the family is fleeting at best. Marco Pantani's parents have to be rescued from a crush of living bodies between the walls of the dead. The supporters then file past place 262 in a long stream. I wait for my turn to stand eye to eye with the box that contains Pantani. Ten seconds at most. Enough to see that a cheap colour print of the man's face has been stuck to the end of his coffin. There he lies, shoved into a wall among the other corpses, one of the finest climbers in the peloton. The stewards keep things moving along and I vacate my spot.

IT'S GETTING ON FOR SIX. The people of the small town of Cesenatico walk back down Via Mazzini, heading home in the rain.

A woman speaks to me from her window. 'This cold is terrible,' she says, and takes my hand. 'And then Marco in his coffin passing so close to my house. It's a sad day.' She lives next door to the barber's shop. A poster in the window reads ADDIO, MARCO, IL

CAMPIONE PER SEMPRE. In the town where he was born, Pantani will be a champion forever. The barber snips at the neck of a customer and flicks away the loose hairs with a soft brush. Black tufts fall on the tiled floor.

In Cesenatico life goes on.

THAT EVENING I SIT DOWN at a table in one of the few open restaurants in the town's deserted streets. I look out of the window at *il porto canale*, a waterway that cuts inland from the Adriatic.

Only a few hours ago on this grey spring day, I had been standing on the quay not far from this spot, surrounded by thousands of Italians who listened with drawn faces to words and music from the church of St Peter the Fisherman, relayed to the crowd through two speakers. The pews inside held a select company: family members, Pantani's closest friends, his teammates and a roll call of cycling greats – Gimondi, Motta, Adorni, Moser, Bugno. Even Charly Gaul, gifted climber and 1958 Tour winner, had made the trip from Luxembourg and received a stirring round of applause for his trouble, when a cycling fan recognised the grizzled old fox and began to shout his name.

As I tuck into my *gnocchi al ragu*, a TV screen high in the corner of the dining room shows non-stop repeats of this afternoon's funeral. Time and again the applause swells as the coffin is carried from the church. The same tearful faces come into view. Pirate flags whip endlessly in the wind and the slow shuffle to the cemetery gates begins anew.

The waiter switches channels. A repeat of the friendly match between Italy and the Czech Republic. It's followed by a popular Italian panel show, presented by a man who patently dyes his hair. He poses the question of the day: who killed Pantani? The tabloids, the authorities that hounded him for a doping confession, his medical staff or a cocaine dealer from Rimini?

I pay my bill and get behind the wheel of my rental car. On my way to the hotel, I make a detour past the cemetery. Via Mazzini is dark and empty. My headlights illuminate the locked cemetery gates. Not a single reminder of the jostling masses at the funeral. No cops, no fans, no flowers, no posters, no candles. There is no all-night vigil for Marco Pantani. He is alone again, just as his life ended in a lonely hotel room down the coast in Rimini.

* * *

THE NEXT MORNING I eat a sweet bun from the hotel's breakfast buffet and check out. I have a 400-kilometre drive ahead of me, north to Bergamo Airport. Driving past the cemetery, I notice that the gate is open and I can't help myself. One last moment with Marco. However many pills he swallowed, however hard he fell, he remains one of the finest climbers in cycling history.

The cement at spot 262 is barely dry. Someone has made a half-arsed attempt to write the name of the dead rider in the soft mortar. Pantani, Marco. This will not be Pantani's final resting place. A family tomb will be built in the shape of a mountain. But for now he has to make do with two red candles in front of his patch of plaster and a vase of yellow tulips.

It's still early and the air is wintry. A handful of people have gathered at the grave. A shivering, grubby-faced man leaning against his bike catches my eye. His name is Peter Mayer and he has cycled down from Austria. A journey of 600 kilometres. 'I really wanted to be at the funeral,' he says. 'But I arrived half a day late. I always thought Pantani was one of the greats. As for what has happened to him? The way I see it, cycling is never going to be squeaky clean.'

The Austrian has spent all of ten minutes at the grave when he climbs back onto his saddle. Time to head home. Later, I pass him on the road and parp my horn. He doesn't recognise me. On the car radio, an Italian weatherwoman is piling on the drama. Snow-drifts are bringing northern Italy to a standstill. Mr Mayer cycles on unaware.

Loners on their bikes can be a little odd. With their manic ap-proach to sport, they hollow out their own bodies. Cold, hunger, thirst, exhaustion, nothing seems to stop them. The rest of the world will never understand their long, debilitating solos.

. . .

MY PLANE ASCENDS AND BANKS ABOVE BERGAMO, but the view is soon snatched away by a thick blanket of cloud. It occurs to me that we will soon be flying over the Alps, Marco Pantani's favoured terrain.

Never again will we see that wiry body of his unleash a punish-ing breakaway. Never again those devastating changes of tempo designed to crush Armstrong. Never again that lightness of touch on the pedals. Or the sweat pouring from that shaved scalp and down past those jug ears. Pantani is no more.

I pick up a sports paper. A colour photograph of the funeral is splashed across the front page. Pantani's coffin borne along on a sea of people. I jump when I see my own bald head a few metres from the coffin. It feels embarrassing somehow. On the pages that follow, I read hundreds of farewell letters by the *tifosi*. You can almost see the tears stain the newsprint, an outpouring of grief that borders on desperation. '*Marco torna. Torna indietro,*' writes Franco on page 7. But Marco is never coming back. He's gone for good.

Little by little, my Dutch sobriety reasserts itself. A stewardess taps me on the shoulder.

'Coffee? Tea?'

That's just how it is. Look after yourself and don't forget your liquids. Coffee, please. Filthy aeroplane coffee. One mouthful and I'm right back down to earth again.

MONA LISA

France

THE SOLDIER STOOD TALL, rifle at the ready. Eyes fixed on a far-off mountain top. Bayonet thrust forward, poised to plunge into the chest of his German foe. Keep driving till you hear the ribs crack.

Mort pour la patrie.

I was cycling slowly and had all the time in the world to take in the statue. How many war memorials were there in France? Every town I passed through had its own version of this helmeted young man with his steely expression. Never a flicker of hesitation in the eyes or a slow stain spreading down the inside leg.

It was late afternoon; 90 minutes since I had dunked my over-heated head into the concrete basin of a public water fountain. Like holding a sizzling pan under the cold tap. I had resurfaced spluttering and coughing.

That exhilarating chill had long since worn off. The heat seemed to be pressing down on me. I could feel my accelerated heart rate thudding in my temples.

It was only when I stood on my pedals that the soldier finally eased out of view. I wondered whether the brake pads might be rubbing against the back wheel. Nonsense. It was just the incline. I looked to the right. The road I had travelled to get here slithered through the valley like a black snake in the grass. I took a swallow from my bottle. My liquid reserves were disappearing fast.

All along the roadside verges, crickets were rubbing their wings together. The shrill sound of an alarm; a mountain on the brink of combustion.

The locals knew the score and spent this time of year 150 kilometres away being fanned by the breezes of the Côte d'Azur. Even the guard dogs posted outside the sparse houses along my route lay dozing in the yard.

I rode over letters that had been daubed on the road surface and partly washed away by the rain. Back to front. I couldn't make them spell a name. Had the Tour de France once passed this way? None of the place names rang a bell with me.

A road sign let me know I had reached an altitude of 825 metres. Still a long way from the summit of the Col de l'Homme Mort, a first-category climb.

I took another slurp from my bottle. Empty. Dense of me not to have mounted a second holder on my frame.

The asphalt continued its climb. No rest for the wicked. No choice but to keep going. Twenty metres further on, a wooden sign shaped like an arrow had been planted at the side of the road. Colourful painted letters read MONA LISA 500M.

Mona Lisa. Strange name for the landscape of Provence. Marie or Christine, fair enough. Jeanne-Marie even, if you wanted a name with more substance. But Mona Lisa? She belonged in Paris, the Louvre to be precise. This way for Leonardo's enigmatic masterpiece.

I passed the sign and looked for something new to focus on.

My last swig from the bottle had done nothing to quench my thirst. My tongue lay parched in my gaping mouth.

In the distance I made out another arrow and struck a deal with myself. Make it to that arrow and I'd make it to the top without a break.

Like the last sign, each letter was painted a different colour. The *A* was the only shape and colour repeated. It reminded me of the watercolours we used to paint with at primary school. More water than colour.

MONA LISA 100M.

This little arrow could lead me to a drinking fountain. Mona Lisa – it might be a garage, a shop selling picture frames, a dealer in truffle oil. I wasn't fussy, as long as there was a cold-water tap. Col de l'Homme Mort would have to wait.

A bigger arrow further along. There she was again: MONA LISA. The letters had doubled in size. And now there was an added clue: LAVANDE. The arrow was pointing down at an angle, urging me off the asphalt road.

A dirt track led down a slope. I dismounted and took small steps, squeezing the brakes as I walked beside my bike. The cleats on the soles of my cycling shoes made the going treacherous.

At the end of the path, an old stone house appeared. The slates on the roof were overgrown with ivy. The battered door was ajar.

'Bonjour,' I said.

Not a sound. Only the monotone chirping of crickets.

'Allo?' I raised my voice but kept my tone hesitant, to make it clear I meant no harm.

No response.

A warped wooden table stood in front of the house. Among bunches of lavender lay a scrap of cardboard with a handwritten message: 'Retour dans quinze minutes'.

I leaned my bike against a tree and pulled my empty bottle from its holder. Back in 15 minutes. Those four words could have been written a while ago. With any luck the owner would reappear before long.

I glanced at my watch. Six o'clock. If I turned around and made a beeline for the hotel I could be in the shower in 90 minutes, all set for a beer and an al fresco dinner. But there was the little matter of today's objective – Dead Man's Pass – to be sorted first.

I circled the house in search of water. Azure shutters barred the windows. Against the wall was a row of impeccably trimmed pots filled with blooming thyme and lavender. Not a tap to be seen. I took off my helmet and left it hanging on my handlebars.

The doorway was hung with plastic strips to stop flies and other pests making an unwelcome entrance. Cautiously I nudged the strips aside with my head.

'Allo ... bonjour?'

My eyes had to adjust to the dark. There was a sickly smell of damp bedclothes.

I stepped inside. The house seemed to consist of one room only. In the corner was a single bed with a tangled sheet. The middle of the room was home to a round metal table and two plastic chairs. A Formica kitchen unit stood against the wall. Complete with tap, thank God.

I began to make out more details. A school map of France on the wall to my left. Routes had been traced on it in pencil. The map was flanked by simple paintings of mountain peaks, some snow-capped, some sun-drenched.

The wall above the bed was plastered top to bottom with photos of cyclists. With one knee resting on the mattress, I took a closer look. The images had been snipped and torn from magazines. I recognised the logo of *Paris Match*. They showed sunlight glinting off bike frames and the sweaty brows of the riders. The skies were the clear blue of my boyhood.

This was a cycling hall of fame. I recognised almost every face: Bahamontes, Indurain, Bartali, Pingeon, Hinault, Simpson, Coppi, Zoetemelk, Pantani, Armstrong, Fuente, Herrera. Here and there, the pictures were interspersed with headlines from French sports paper *L'Équipe*.

Whoever lived here must be a cycling fanatic.

I walked over to the sink. A back wheel with a flat tyre was leaning against a cupboard door. Under the sink was a clutch of inner tubes, a black tangle of lifeless eels. I bent closer to see what kind of valve they had.

'Bonjour, monsieur!'

A shrill surprise. I spun around to see a large woman in the doorway. The plastic strips fell like dreadlocks around her head. She stepped into the room, neatly skirting the table and chairs.

I began to make out her features. An oval face, creased forehead and long curtains of red hair that fell to either side, parted along a line of grey.

'Je suis Lisa.'

Her smile was a little forced.

I shook her hand and was about to launch into an explanation for walking into her house uninvited. But she spoke before I did.

'What's the trouble? Flat tyre? Gears acting up? Or do you need a pair of pliers to adjust the brakes? Just say the word.'

I held up my bottle.

'Empty.'

The woman took the bottle from my hand, walked over to the tap and filled it to the brim. She put it down on the table in the middle of the room.

'Allez, take a seat. Let me give you something better to drink. Water is for plants.'

She yanked aside a curtain in front of an open cupboard and pulled out a carafe of dark juice, which she put on the table along with two glasses.

'Blueberry. Good for your bowels.'

I sat down, feeling I had no choice but to obey this woman in her own domain.

We drank our juice without a word. I looked at her over my glass. Rosy complexion, a faceful of freckles, bare shoulders and strong arms. There was a twinkle in her eyes, but her stiff movements and wrinkled skin told me she must at least be pushing 60.

'Where are you heading?'

'I'm staying not far from Sault.'

She threw her head back and drained the last drops from her glass. The top button of her flowery dress was open, announcing breasts that definitely qualified as a bosom.

'What's your gear ratio?'

'50–34 and 13–26.'

She peered under the table and studied my bare legs, then took in the rest of me before her gaze settled on my face.

'I can't let you go in this state. You'll never make it.'

Lisa marched over to her kitchen. She filled a pot with water, put it on the hob and lit the gas with one strike of the match.

'Quite a collection you've got there,' I said, pointing at the photos.

While she looked at the wall, she poked her gums with the end of the extinguished match.

'I know those men like the back of my hand. Everything about them: best performances, frame size, heart rate at rest and during exertion, habits, family tree, trials and tribulations.'

Lisa slotted the match into the gap between her front teeth. She slid it in and out, examined the pickings, then tossed it in the ashtray and sat back down.

I took another gulp of juice, got up and walked over to the photos. I felt the urge to test her. Was this woman some kind of fantasist or did she really know her cycling?

'That's Miguel Indurain. Right?'

She tilted her head to see which photo I was pointing at. 'Ah, yes. Miguel. That long streak of piss from Pamplona. Won the Tour de France five times in a row. The way he left world champion LeMond for dead on that final climb up to Luz Ardiden in 1990. Poetry in motion. Light touch on the handlebars, pushing a heavy gear. When I saw that little crease in Miguel's neck, I knew he was having a good day.'

She turned her attention to the pot on the cooker.

She had passed my test. I remembered that duel in the mountains. Indurain at his mightiest.

Lisa tore open a packet of spaghetti and slid the contents into the boiling water.

'Let's get some carbs down you. Get that engine of yours going again.'

I didn't dare say no. Besides, she was right: I had been running on empty. Could she tell just by looking at me?

'I only wanted to fill my bottle and get back on the road.'

'I know what a man on a bike needs,' she said.

She was standing with her back to me. The sluggish sway of her backside made it clear she was stirring in the pan.

I stepped outside. The sun was sinking but the heat hadn't let up. My bike was up against the tree. I pressed a button on the computer. Distance: 41.7 kilometres. That's how far I was from my hotel. If I stayed to eat, I'd be late back. And of course, there was still l'Homme Mort to attend to.

'Grub's up!' Lisa shouted.

I wandered back inside.

The air was heavy with the damp of freshly drained pasta. Over by the sink, Lisa tipped the spaghetti onto two plates and poured a jar of red sauce over the top. She stirred the two together with a few supple flicks of the wrist and put the plates on the table.

'Eat,' she said. It was an order.

She fetched two glasses and an open bottle of wine. She filled the glasses and raised a toast.

'To the cyclists of the world,' she said.

We ate and drank in silence. My stomach growled as I took my first mouthfuls.

Once she had cleared her plate, she began to speak.

'My husband was a cyclist. Jean Hochon. You wouldn't know him. Local rider, no great shakes. Never won a prize. Worked full-time at the abattoir, had to get his training in at the crack of dawn. You'll never get anywhere with a regime like that.'

She took the empty plates over to the sink. The spaghetti lay heavy on my stomach, but I could feel my energy rising. Yes, time to pick up my bottle and get back on the bike. I rose to my feet. Lisa came and stood next to me.

'Lie down on the bed.'

She sounded like she meant business.

'Er, I really just wanted to pay you for that lovely meal and ...'

'Go on, lie down. Let Lisa finish her work.'

Granted, I had been so bold as to sneak into her house unin-vited and nose around. Not exactly polite, but surely I was under no obligation to stay?

Lisa continued to point at the bed. 'I know how tough l'Homme Mort is,' she said.

It was the determined look on that oval face of hers that made me crumble. What was I letting myself in for? Was she planning to pray for me? This was a Catholic heartland after all.

I did the decent thing and removed my cycling shoes. I placed them next to the bed and slowly lay down on my back. Cobwebs clung to the window frame. The sheets felt clammy. I wasn't the first man to lie here. These sheets smelled of man sweat.

'Where's your husband, if you don't mind me asking? Does he still cycle?'

She walked over to the sink and produced an aerosol can from behind a couple of pots. She shook it wildly.

'Jean is dead. Has been 20 years. He came down with an infection at the abattoir. Injured himself while boning a carcass. His arm turned hard and blue. They admitted him to hospital in Carpentras with a raging fever and three days later he was dead. Severe blood poisoning, they said.'

She sat down next to me on the bed and slipped off my white ankle socks. I thought of my grubby toenails and felt a stab of shame, but Lisa didn't seem to notice.

'He may not have been much of a cyclist,' Mona Lisa said with a dreamy look in her eyes, 'but he had the finest pair of legs in the region. He was proud of them himself. I shaved them every other day. The old-fashioned way, cut-throat razor and warm soapy lather. I can still hear that lovely scraping sound on his skin, like it was yesterday. Jean couldn't stand it when the stubble peeped through. Neither could I, to be honest. A rider's wife can't make love to her man if all she can feel are those hairs pricking into her soft flesh.'

She gave the aerosol another good shake and began to spray. White foam spurted over my brown legs. With a smooth touch, she spread it till both legs were completely covered.

'Now lie still for a minute or two.'

What was this stuff good for? The smell put me in mind of hospital disinfectant. Or perhaps it was a kind of tiger balm. I waited for a glowing sensation to kick in.

On the wall above me, Lucho Herrera was climbing a steep road in the polka-dot jersey, cheered on by bare-chested supporters. Fists clenched, they screamed at their mountain king, who was still breathing steadily despite the thin air. Herrera. The pint-sized Colombian could barely keep up with the peloton during the flat stages of the Tour de France. It was only in the mountains that he felt at home, free of the jitters and the jostling in the pack. He wasn't made for riding bar to bar. He was, as climbers so often are, a loner on two wheels.

Lisa returned, holding a towel that dripped with water. She draped it across my thighs and rubbed my legs down with a firm hand.

'Voilà!' she exclaimed.

The hairs on my legs had disappeared with the foam. Beneath my tanned skin I saw veins I could not recall having seen so clearly before.

What had I been so afraid of? Lisa knew what she was doing. She went over to a cupboard and I heard the clink of bottles. I turned my head and saw her screw the top off a bottle that held a clear green liquid.

'What's that?' I asked.

'My little secret,' said Lisa. She poured it over my hairless legs and I felt the greasy liquid trickle and tickle. I inhaled the smell of eucalyptus and lifted my head from the pillow to see what she was doing. Her fleshy hands began to rub the concoction into my thighs and calves.

'They've all lain here on this bed. All the big names on that wall. Herrera. I could feel how his meat was attached to his bones. Pork tenderloins, bulging in the middle and growing tougher towards either end. He always fell asleep under my hands. Not that we had much to say to each other, him with his Spanish, me with my local twang. An impossible combination. But my hands and his legs understood each other.'

I let my head fall back onto the pillow and felt another shot of the clear green liquid gush over my leg. With perfect timing she lifted it up. The liquid ran over my skin and with one swift motion she rubbed it into the back of my thighs before a single drop touched the sheets.

'Then there was Bernard Hinault, that crazy Breton. He liked it rough. Skin so thick, flesh so tough that I had to press my thumbs deep to get at the muscles. *"Plus fort, plus fort!"* he would shout. A wild man, that Hinault.'

A strange chuckle came from deep within her, much higher than her normal voice.

She took one calf then the other between thumb and forefinger and rubbed the oil towards the knee. It was as if she was teasing out the blood that had collected in the muscle. It was painful, but the pain felt good.

'Koblet. A first-class jessie if ever there was one. Handsome Hugo they used to call him. Always had a comb tucked away in his jersey. But scraggy as goat's meat to the touch. When I massaged him, little ridges of dirt would form beneath my fingertips. A rider who didn't wash. You're nice and clean. Sweaty, but it's clean sweat. Cycling sweat. No smell quite like it.'

Lisa wiped her hands on her dress and went and stood in the middle of the room. She picked up the box of matches and lit a large, half-melted candle that stood on the table. The flickering glow lit up her face and sent her wrinkles rippling.

I stifled a yawn. The air was thick and warm in here. Lisa returned to the bed and sat down beside me. 'Fausto Coppi, he was my favourite. Soft meat in the calves, every fibre saturated with blood. I always took my time with Fausto, the sweetheart. Strolling down the path to our house with his bike at his side, he would whistle that song about Mona Lisa.'

She began to sing softly, in hopeless English. It was all I could do to make out the words. My eyelids grew heavy. She began to rub my thighs. Lisa took the largest muscle in both hands, pressed gently and let her hands slide up to my crotch. A motion she repeated again and again.

I let her do her thing and felt the weariness being squeezed from my legs. They seemed lighter somehow. Coppi. Didn't the Italian champion have his own faithful masseur? Biagio Cavanna. A shambling figure with a stick and dark glasses. A blind man feeling his way through the world of cycling. But when he inhaled the smell of massage oil and touched the legs of his Fausto, Cavanna knew exactly where he needed to be in that warren of muscle and sinew.

There was no suppressing my yawns. This was a battle with sleep.

Lisa rubbed the skin of my thighs. They were glowing. The scent of eucalyptus filled the room.

I had to keep her talking. Falling asleep would be a step too far. This woman was a complete stranger to me. Besides, I still had a long cycle back to the hotel. I tried to focus. Did all those riders come here to train in the mountains? Bahamontes came from Toledo, Pantani from Italy. Why come all this way?

Lisa strolled back over to the table. She grabbed the wine bottle and took another swig.

'Lisa, what brought all those famous climbers here?'

She came and stood beside me. Red patches had appeared on her throat and her upper arms. Her voice softened. 'Too many questions, *mon ami*. Enjoy, just as those who came before you enjoyed.'

I tried to formulate a new question. I mean, Coppi ... How could Coppi have lain on this bed for heaven's sake? He died in 1960, the second of January. A date that had lodged in my mind since reading his biography.

'Lisa, did you meet Coppi when he was alive?' I asked drowsily. 'How old *are* you?'

I began to count.

She poured more eucalyptus oil on my legs. I felt it dribble down the inside of my left thigh. A familiar itch. I was too tired to scratch.

Lisa's voice dropped to a whisper. 'They are afraid in the mountains. Afraid to be alone, afraid like all of us. I give them my smile and they overcome their fear. Once you have lain on this bed, no harm will come to you. Every rider knows.'

Her hands glided over my thighs. My muscles felt softer than ever. I tried to sit up but my fingers found no purchase on the slick mattress. I tensed my arms, my abdominals, and for a second I seemed to be rising.

My eyes narrowed to slits. Lisa brushed her hair out of her face with her oily fingers and loosened another button on her dress. Then another. Her bosom was hanging free in her slip, beads of sweat making her décolleté gleam in the candlelight. A dark wave sloshed through my head, the muscles in my arms seemed to melt. There was nothing to do but let go. Floating then falling. Deeper than ever before.

How long had I been out for?

The candle on the table gave just enough light for me to make out the photos above me. Lucho Herrera was still eating up the same steep stretch of mountain. His fans continued to spur him on. Chromed spokes shone in a wheel that was no longer turning.

Heavy breathing next to the bed. I rolled over and inhaled a heady mix of sweat, eucalyptus and booze breath.

Lisa must have fallen asleep on the floor. She lay on her side. The straps of her slip had fallen from her shoulders and her hands were clamped between her bare thighs. The biggest foetus I had ever seen.

Slowly I eased my shoulders off the mattress. Her flowery dress lay like a crumpled dishcloth beside my pillow. I swung around and sat on the edge of the bed. My feet touched down on the floor next to Lisa's sleeping face. The red wine must have made countless circuits through her body by now. I took a closer look at her and saw a young woman's smile lighting up an old face. The longer I looked, the more it seemed to widen into a mellow grin; sardonic, blissful.

I padded past her sleeping, half-naked body. She reminded me of a loyal dog that had lost its hunting instinct but still slept close to its master.

Reaching the table, I picked up my filled water bottle. Water, that was how all this had started. I took the precaution of blowing out the candle.

'*Merci*, Lisa,' I whispered in the darkness.

I shuffled towards the door with arms outstretched to make sure I didn't bump into anything. The contours of my bike were visible through the plastic strips in the doorway. It was a clear night, the moon was shining down. The day's heat lingered on, though thankfully less oppressive than it had been inside. I slid my bottle into its holder, took the helmet from my handlebars and put it on. Walking my bike up the path, I took my first steps on the loose stones. I was worried the crunch might wake Lisa but the house remained quiet.

When I reached the asphalt road, I swung my right leg over the saddle and clicked my shoe into the pedal. I couldn't see very far ahead. To the left was the downhill ride to the hotel, to the right the climb to the Col de l'Homme Mort.

I had slept soundly. There was water in my bottle. I had eaten my fill and my legs were well oiled.

What was it Lisa had said to me as I had drifted off to sleep on her bed? 'Lie on this bed and no harm will come to you.'

I headed right.

My eyes, heavy with sleep, followed the white stripe on the asphalt. I was moving nicely. The big gear I was grinding didn't hurt at all.

The colours of the mountain began to change. The trees and bushes thinned out. By the side of the road I saw a sign: COL DE L'HOMME MORT OUVERT. Of course the pass was open. This peak was mine for the taking.

It was dark. No lights on my bike. But an auspicious moon lit up the flank of the mountain. My legs did everything I asked of them. I changed up a cog to get better traction on the pedals.

No signs to point the way, no houses, no people. The Dead Man was a silent mountain. My legs were glowing. And before I knew where I was, the one sign I wanted to see appeared at the side of the road. Name and altitude: COL DE L'HOMME MORT, 1163 MÈTRES.

I had reached the top.

Satisfied, I dismounted and grabbed my full bottle. The water tasted different to the water at the hotel. Sweeter. Lampposts picked out the road in the valley but there was no telling where Lisa's house might be.

A chilly breeze blew me wide awake but had no effect on my legs. They continued to glow. I drained my bottle. My lips widened to a grin all by themselves.

Back on the saddle, I began my descent in the dark. The wind whistled around me but that stupid grin was there to stay.

I sang out in a single surge of breath. Her name was carried from mountain to mountain.

I called to her again and again, stretching every syllable.

Li-sa. Mo-na Li-ii-sa.

She was alone with her riders. From the saddle, they all gazed down on Lisa. May no harm ever come to her. Lisa belonged with her climbers. And now she belonged with me too.

CYCLING PORN

Spain

FEDERICO BAHAMONTES HAS SHUT UP SHOP. Business at his bicycle store in the historic heart of Toledo had been slow for some time and, after nearly half a century, it was time for Spain's 1959 Tour de France winner to call it a day. The premises now belong to a wholesaler in brightly coloured plastic tat. Made in China.

The news came from a friend of mine, a Spanish correspondent who had interpreted for me back in 2003 when I filmed a portrait of 'Baha'. It saddens me to think the store is no more. Change is all well and good, but some places in this world should forever stay the same.

The finest moniker ever dreamt up for a cyclist was dreamt up for Bahamontes: the Eagle of Toledo. When I went to see him, he was still looking impressive at 74. Slender, well groomed, perfumed almost. Distinguished grey hair. Gold-framed spectacles perched on an imposing nose.

Bahamontes gave me a tour of the place. The showroom was light and airy, mainly stocked with children's bikes. Racing bikes were in the minority. A big black-and-white photograph hanging on a pillar showed the tens of thousands who had gathered in the shadow of the cathedral on Toledo's main square to celebrate his Tour victory. The bicycle store had opened its doors that same summer.

The lady at the cash register with the frosty allure of a marble bust turned out to be Baha's wife Fermina. Face taut, dyed red hair scraped back on her head. A hundred hands could not warm her. Their faithful helper Faustino was there too. In 1959 he had walked into the store as a 13-year-old and saw the mechanics tinkering with the bikes back in the workshop. Faustino became fascinated with the technical side of the racing bike and before long he was taken on as an apprentice.

For 50 years, it was Faustino everyone went to for valves, screws, spokes, a saddle or oil to grease their chain. When I was there, his left arm was in a sling. He had cut himself closing a window. No reason to pull a sickie. He was perfectly capable of helping customers find a new bike one-handed.

Bahamontes was not the kind of man to serve in a shop on a daily basis. It was never that busy in any case. He'd much rather gad about in his flashy Mercedes. He confided that he was only keeping the place going for Faustino. Bahamontes planned to wait till his faithful assistant reached pensionable age before giving the place up.

While Faustino and Señora Bahamontes stood out front like showroom dummies come to life, Bahamontes walked me through to the back. At first we sat in his little office. A stone eagle in the cabinet behind him had spread its wings and looked like it might swoop down and settle on its namesake's shoulder at any moment.

The walls were hung with photos of Bahamontes the climber. He liked nothing better than to take off on his own during the mountain stages. One famous anecdote claimed that in the 1954 Tour de France he was so far ahead of his rivals on the Col de Romeyère that he got off his bike and treated himself to an ice cream, only jumping back on the saddle when the second rider came over the top.

Not quite true, apparently. Bahamontes was happy to set the record straight. 'I was in the middle of a solo on the mountain when one of the official cars rammed me. My derailleur was smashed and my team leader was nowhere to be seen, so I dismounted. I saw an ice cream cart, one with two big holes in the counter. There was no one minding it, so I shoved one hand in, smeared some ice cream into my bottle and polished it off while I was waiting for help to arrive.'

From his office, he led me through to the old workshop. A drab room with dozens of pliers, cutters, saws and hammers on the wall, all shapes and sizes. Bahamontes rummaged around in an alcove and pulled out his winner's jersey from 1959. It was a genuine thrill to stroke that legendary yellow. Wool that prickled. Itchy stitches.

Bahamontes moved on to the bike he had won the Tour with. He suspended the old frame from a couple of cables and began to speak to it softly. He turned the pedals and let the chain slide over the cogs. The sound tickled my ears.

The Eagle spoke to his legendary two-wheeler: 'You always showed your spirit, that's what won us the Tour. You and I. We were a couple, we were roommates. When we were leading the way through the mountains, all they could do was stare at our backsides.'

Bahamontes's left hand glided across the frame to touch the worn gear stick. Gently, he eased it back and the chain leapt across the five cogs. He squirted thick oil on the moving parts.

While Fermina presided over the cash desk out in the shop, Bahamontes shamelessly made love to his old bike. Soft porn, cycling porn. In sultry Spanish, the Eagle of Toledo told the helplessly hanging frame, 'I always brought you to my hotel room. So you could be close to me.'

The Eagle's bicycle store is no more. Bahamontes had to carry his winning bike from 1959 out onto the square like a bride across the threshold. Where are they now, Baha and his bike? I hope they have headed into the mountains. Lying exhausted at the roadside after a punishing climb. The cheek of Baha's distinguished face pressed to the saddle, his arms tenderly embracing the frame.

Sleeping soundly together.